MASTERING

THE

UNIVERSE

MASTERING THE UNIVERSE

THE OBSCENE WEALTH OF THE RULING CLASS, WHAT THEY DO WITH THEIR MONEY, AND WHY YOU SHOULD HATE THEM EVEN MORE

ROB LARSON

Haymarket Books
Chicago, Illinois

Published in 2024 by
Haymarket Books
P.O. Box 180165
Chicago, IL 60618
www.haymarketbooks.org

ISBN: 979-8-88890-085-7

Distributed to the trade in the US through Consortium Book Sales and Distribution (www.cbsd.com) and internationally through Ingram Publisher Services International (www.ingramcontent.com).

This book was published with the generous support of Lannan Foundation, Wallace Action Fund, and Marguerite Casey Foundation.

Special discounts are available for bulk purchases by organizations and institutions. Please email info@haymarketbooks.org for more information.

Cover design by David Gee.
Illustration of Earth © 2014 Dmitry Rukhlenko.

Printed in Canada by union labor.

Library of Congress Cataloging-in-Publication data is available.

10 9 8 7 6 5 4 3 2 1

To Noam, whose work we carry on

CONTENTS

This is an impressive crowd—the haves and the have-mores. Some people call you the elites; I call you my base.
—**George W. Bush**[1]

I saw that mill built stone by stone; I saw the pickers, the carding engines, the spinning mules and looms put into it, one after the other, and I would see every machine and stone crumble to the floor and fall again before I would accede to your wishes.
—**Colonel Richard Borden,**[2] **cotton baron, on the thirteen-hour day**

The only thing for which we can combine is the underlying ideal of Socialism; justice and liberty.
—**George Orwell**[3]

BOSS FIGHT

The world's billionaires now have their own private space programs. The classic public space services like NASA were paid for by aggressive taxes on the rich, but those are gone now so Jeff Bezos, Elon Musk, and Richard Branson each have their own, where they take their friends to orbit, soak up media coverage, and even pretend to do research.[1] The wealth gap has reached such towering proportions that the most insanely expensive projects are now within the play budgets of our fun-hoarding ruling class.

Conservative novelist Tom Wolfe coined the term "masters of the universe" to refer to elite Wall Street financiers, and it became a broader mainstream term for the insanely rich elites of today and their fantasies of power.[2] But when things actually turn ugly, it's another story—the Masters had their hands out for bailouts after the 2008 and 2023 financial crises, and when the COVID-19 pandemic took hold in 2020 they stampeded out of town to their remote estates and summer homes.

And their decisions matter. A leaked 2005 investment memo from two Citibank economists called the US a "plutonomy," meaning "economic growth is powered by and largely consumed by the wealthy few." They estimated that "the top 1% of households . . . account for 33% of net worth," compared to "the rest, the 'non-rich,' the multitudinous many, but only accounting for surprisingly small

bites of the economic pie." They concluded that for their business, "clearly, the analysis of the top 1% of US households is para-
mount."[3] Many Americans, encouraged to imagine themselves as
billionaires-to-be, may hope to enter the 1 percent, but it's a tough
lift at $4.4 million American just to get in, let alone the average of
$10.4 million in wealth you'll need to really fit in.[4]

Meanwhile, incomes have stagnated for most of the US population for decades and debt has risen steeply, while the real fruits
of economic growth went to the top households. And in an incredible development, the average life expectancy in the US, the richest
country in the world, actually stopped rising in 2015. It fell until
2018, then rose briefly only to drop again with the pandemic, continuing through 2021.[5] That same year, the billionaires' hoard went
from $3 trillion to $4.5 trillion.[6]

And today's data shows that every country, no matter how
poor or rich, has a hyper-affluent tiny ruling class. As the *Financial
Times* put it, the world is in "a new imperial age" with "a system of
indirect rule that has involved the integration of leaders of developing countries into the network of the new ruling class."[7] That class
is more worldwide in its lifestyle than ever, since its members frequently count among their wealth a significant passport collection,
purchased from the many countries that offer full or partial citizenship in exchange for making a qualifying real estate purchase or
other investment.[8] Safes stuffed with global residency documents
are the family jewels of the world's ruling class.

As we behold continents on fire, pandemics thrashing public health systems to smithereens, and falling economic prospects
and life spans, we must remember one thing: All this, *all this* is for
the benefit of a tiny number of people, a small class that owns the
wealth and institutions of the economy, a ruling class for whom we
are ruining every part of the natural systems on Earth, and screw-
ing over a gigantic social majority that's desperate for a fair share of
the wealth they produce in the first place.

As billionaire investor Warren Buffett said, "There is class warfare, all right, but it's my class, the rich class, that's making war, and we're winning."[9]

The wider world gets peeks at the wealth of the ruling class when parts of it get in trouble, like when Russian oligarchs had their megayachts, private planes, and other assets seized due to Western sanctions during the Russo-Ukrainian War. But there are so many more exploits to explore, and elite-class vulnerabilities to learn. This book is for learning all about our global rogues' gallery of remote ruling-class bastards.

WHY READ ABOUT THE RULING CLASS?

I f you're the type that's out to envy the flashy high-end lifestyle of the rich, there's no shortage of magazines to read and online videos you can watch. Countries like the US that celebrate wealthy people are happy to produce tons of media around them, from *Downton Abbey* to *Succession*. The rich of the real world have their luxurious lives depicted in *Lifestyles of the Rich and Famous* and the *Wall Street Journal*'s Mansion section.

But this book is not just for ogling the velvet lives of the ruling class, although there's plenty of room for that. It's about taking the rich out of the cockpit of society and putting a democratic system in their place. Because beyond their multiple gigantic homes and private jet miles, the control of the ruling class over the rest of us is pretty stunning, not to mention utterly grossly undeserved.

It's a fact that today eight rich men own as much wealth as the bottom 50 percent of the world's population (all four billion plus of them).[1] In 2020, half the names on the *Forbes* list of the fifty richest families had appeared on the list in 1983.[2] The richest 1 percent of US households owns 40 percent of the stock market, and the top 10 percent owns *84 percent*, meaning that the rich own corporate America and its great productive power.[3] These figures are pretty

1

obscene, and a peek behind the high-tech security fences protecting their enclaves reveals a lifestyle even obscener.

The overpowering flow of money to these families has led to some unbelievably dumb and cartoonishly wasteful uses of the wealth of humanity. On Wall Street, it's now somewhat out of fashion but still common for rich finance employees to literally eat gold, using a topping on their desserts and coffees that could completely change the lives of the less fortunate.[4] Other members of the ruling class think big, like when billionaire Larry Ellison bought one of the Hawaiian islands in 2013.[5] Despite Hawaii having the highest rents in the US, Ellison gave makeovers to elite resorts there instead of building affordable housing.

Today's giant megayachts burn a hundred gallons of diesel an hour standing still, and customizations include Kevlar-lined safe rooms.[6] The richest tenth of the world is responsible for almost half of all climate emissions, playing a giant, disproportionate role in climate change and destroying the ecosystem, even while portraying themselves as environmental celebrity spokesmen.[7] As you research the ruling class, you discover that getting rid of them isn't just something needed for humanity to progress, it's a matter of life and death.

They have surprising numbers of apartments they've never lived in, expensive clothes they do not wear, imported cars they do not drive. And it is all paid for with money the rest of the population is desperate for—there are many thousands of GoFundMe fundraising appeals for groceries and rent for working-class people, enough that the platform created a separate category for monthly expenses and bills.[8]

So this book isn't just for leering at the gross excesses of the elite lifestyle, or feeling the heat of watching cruelly hoarded money wasted on tacky-ass conspicuous consumption. This book is for fighting back—organizing your coworkers into unions to wrestle the boss for a fair share, building political movements to demand universal health care and good schools anyone's kid can go to. And it's for helping to take late action to preserve a version of our natural environment and climate for future generations. To achieve anything, important labor and environmental movements require a good understanding of what's going on—including the shifting strategies of the owning class and their corporate property.

The point of this book is not just to study the rich, but to learn their vulnerabilities, and to help build the growing movements that could put some limits back on the power of the ruling class that owns our economy and runs the government. In the past the rich have had what they consider punishing tax rates slapped on their giant incomes, the popular voting franchise was established over their objection, and agitation even forced some of their corporate monopolies to be broken up. And even in a country as capitalist as the United States, the rich have experienced one major *expropriation*, a massive seizure of their productive wealth that was worth the equivalent of billions today.

That time was the emancipation of the American slaves in 1863. And one good emancipation deserves another.

Overview

How can some dumb book help accomplish all that? We'll start by looking at the money, digging into who has how much, the ruling class's share of the total economy, and with a special interest in the 1 percent's ownership of the corporate world of big business. Knowing just how much wealth our rulers are hoarding tells us how much is available to be put to way-better use. Before we get to the lurid lifestyles and ugly class conflict, we need to learn who's holding the bag, and chapter 1 shows us just that for the US and around the world.

The second chapter turns to the steamy, secretive world of the ruling-class lifestyle. Gigantic homes, private planes, purposeless expensive trinkets, and of course an entourage of groveling ass-kissers are just the beginning. Yachts with Picassos, billion-dollar divorces—it's all here, and it's all disgusting.

Next we take a microscope to the class structure of our society, considering what defines different economic and social classes and how they relate to each other. A picture emerges quickly of concentrated wealth forcing the working class to toil for corporate empires. Understanding that today's global companies enrich themselves by exploiting the labor of the working class also reveals the potential power of the toiling majority: the boss needs us more than we need the boss. The segregated economic lives we lead are also part of the class landscape profiled in chapter 3.

Chapter 4 takes up the tired defenses of the rich rolled out by various bootlicking sycophants. According to supporters of capitalism, the richest families deserve their monumental fortunes for all kinds of dumb meritless reasons: more productive personal characteristics, natural selection among people, alleged technological innovations, and above all philanthropic charitable giving. Every one of these embarrassing fig leaves wilts the minute you look at it critically, and yet few prominent media figures seem to ever criticize their bosses, allowing these bald-faced lies to sink into the popular consciousness. Hastening the decay of these "common-sense" myths is a direct aid to the growth of social movements to build a better world, since belief in them is often the first thing organizers have to toil against.

Our fifth chapter is a careful consideration of the ecological impact of the 1 percent. Despite often claiming to be Very Concerned About the Environment, wealthy businesspeople, politicians, and celebrities have the most disgracefully wasteful lifestyles in the world, scarfing down resources and farting out wildly disproportionate levels of climate emissions. The public data on this subject is pretty stunning, and ought to serve as a handy road map to preventing our so-called betters from continuing to cook the planet.

Chapter 6 explores the numerous ruling-class subspecies, first reviewing key ruling-class industries like Wall Street and Silicon Valley, and then governing elites around the world. Russian oligarchs, Chinese billionaires, European corporate families, Arab monarchs—this chapter takes a trip around the world and dissects every specimen of owning-class jerk known to science.

Finally, chapter 7 starts with the resurrection of the labor movement and the stunning upswing in support for socialism in the US. As we'll see, socialism as a goal goes beyond the highly popular but relatively modest reforms associated with the cause today, like Medicare for All. Real socialism means expropriation of the great wealth of the ruling class, from its vast pools of liquid wealth to its tightly held ownership of corporate America. Not just taxing their giant incomes, but actually confiscating the assets that put them in charge of society would be the break with capitalism that past reform efforts failed to make. Doing so would allow us to operate the economy on a democratic model with gains for all, rather than enriching the wealthy while we toil for a pittance in dead-end jobs. So with the working class rediscovering its strength, this final chapter puts on the brass knuckles and talks about what it'll really take to pry the invisible hand of the ruling class off the steering wheel of society.

You can't overthrow a ruling class you know nothing about. Grab a beverage and put up your feet, you'll soon have the secret access ports of the Death Star of capitalism, and then the clock's ticking till the big finale.

CHAPTER 1

THE NUMBERS

JUST HOW RICH ARE WE TALKING?

I can't live on 5 percent or 6 percent return on my
investments anymore. It's not enough. I need more.
—**Wealth peer group participant**[1]

God gave me my money.
—**John D. Rockefeller**[2]

Even people who rarely think about the economy are aware of their country's billionaires. The richest people around the world are often treated as symbols of the people's hopes for prosperity, or as national champions. Famous ones get celebrity-level news coverage of their cosmetic surgery and high-stakes divorces. But beyond that, Americans don't talk that much about class—the sociologist Paul Blumberg called it "America's forbidden thought."[3]

However, Americans' intuitions about the wealth gap were fascinatingly revealed by a study conducted by Harvard Business School and Duke University.[4] A representative national sample was asked to estimate what they thought the US wealth distribution was, and then to indicate what they felt an ideal distribution might look like. The researchers found Americans believe that the wealthiest 20 percent of households own about 59 percent of total US wealth, while the number was closer to 84 percent when the study was conducted. Their ideal distributions of wealth had the richest fifth of the country owning a relatively modest 32 percent—closer to Sweden's distribution. Despite reliable media opposition to any suggestion of redistribution of wealth, they found "much more consensus than disagreement" on the subject.

But when you're talking about millions and billions of dollars, it can sometimes feel overwhelming or totally abstract to learn about how much wealth exists in society, and how much is stuffed right at the top. It can feel like trying to think about how much water is in the ocean, how many stars are in the galaxy, or how old the Earth is. But knowing the details is important, I think, especially down the road when we look at where the money goes. And if you want to do something about the wealth and power of the rich, you need to at least understand them and their holdings. Especially because it's not just cash—other economic assets are also locked in the hands of the rich, like stock in the corporations we buy from and work for. Social control, like money, can be hoarded at the top.

But just how much money are we talking about here?

Making Payroll

We can measure up the money of a society in different ways. One way is by income—who earns how much of the total income, and from what kind of economic activity. For the large majority of us, incomes play the main role in deciding our standard of living, since most people don't have large amounts of independent wealth.

Economists studying incomes in the US and around the world have identified clear historical patterns. Incomes broadly grew slowly over the long historical eras from antiquity to the industrial revolution of the 1700s and 1800s, as hard-won gains with simple technological advances were wiped out by periodic

plagues, wars, and climatic shifts. With the arrival of the Industrial Revolution, production of goods grew and national incomes
rose in Western countries through the Gilded Age of Rockefeller
and Carnegie, then fell with the Great Depression and the destruction of so much wealth in the world wars. Production and total
national incomes then rose again in the postwar era of more gov-
ernment-managed growth.

Through this long history, however, different families had
very different economic experiences. Sticking to incomes for now,
for the working majority wages fell during the Industrial Revolution as workers were pushed off farms and into factories, in harsh
competition with one another, thus creating today's modern labor
market of wage-based work. In the late 1800s, incomes finally grew
for some workers, as labor broadly became more skill-based, and
as the professional middle class of managers, engineers, and other
educated professionals grew to support the fast-growing industri-
alizing economy.[5]

But incomes for rich households rose strongly through the
Industrial Revolution as large existing merchant fortunes or traditional landholdings could be invested in capital for industry. And
income grew quickly for owners of that physical capital—productive assets like factories, farms, oil refineries, and data centers. But
since capital ownership has always been far more concentrated
than people's ability to labor, this growth mainly benefited the
richest. Over this period top household incomes went from being
predominantly based on land rents and commerce to being primarily from financial assets that represent ownership of big business, and the data reveals that to this day within the top 1 percent
of households "pure capital income (rent, interests, and dividends)
clearly predominates."[6]

This means a lot of the shifting fortunes of historical struggles
among the classes can be seen in the factor share of income, which
refers to how much of the total national income goes to the owners
of different "factors of production"—labor, capital, or important

natural resources like oil or lithium. The Industrial Revolution in seventeenth- and eighteenth-century Europe slowly lifted capital's share of income to a peak of 40 percent in 1870, which then gradually declined and fell more steeply after World War II, before rising again in all countries after the 1980s' turn to "neoliberalism," the current version of capitalism characterized by free markets, reduced social welfare spending, limited labor unions, and much lower taxes on the rich.[7]

This income history is documented by contemporary economists like Thomas Piketty, the French economic historian and breakout publishing success. Piketty, for his part, was a professed liberal at the time of his famous book *Capital in the Twenty-First Century*, supporting capitalism but with traditional "social democratic" measures—a progressive income and estate tax, regulations on industries, extensive public services. Despite his support for profits and markets, he got so uncomfortable looking at a wealth gap as big as today's that he wrote a gigantic book about it.

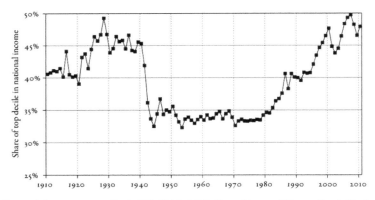

Figure 1. Income inequality in US, 1910–2010. From Thomas Piketty, *Capital in the Twenty-First Century* (Cambridge, MA: Belknap Press, 2014).

One reliable pattern throughout history is that inequality of labor income in wages or salaries is modest compared to the giant inequality of ownership of capital. Ownership of these productive assets creates its own flow of passive capital income. And while the modern US is famous for its high-paid CEOs, the fact remains that for the very richest families, capital income dominates. Piketty finds "the upper centile [1 percent] always consists of several different social groups, some with very high incomes from capital and others with very high incomes from labor; the latter do not supplant the former."[8] But as we'll see later in this chapter, the really crucial distinction of the rich is their ownership of most financial assets, including most of the stock in corporate America, meaning their shareholder capital and incomes are what most distinguish them as a class.

Piketty's book is full of great insights, but maybe the most fascinating analysis of US incomes came from the RAND Corporation, the famous Pentagon-associated private think tank. In 2018 two of their researchers conducted a simple "counterfactual," a what-if scenario for the economy, that imagined what today's wealth disparity would be like if incomes grew evenly across tax brackets. This question was spurred on by the fact that over the big-government New Deal period, from World War II until the 1980s, incomes in the US had grown in exactly this way.[9] This growth tended to track the growth of the overall economy, so while the rich remained wealthier than the rest of us, incomes grew at about the same pace, partly because labor unions granted some collective bargaining power to working-class people.

This relative equality ended when the New Deal order was replaced by the pro-market policies of the present neoliberal era— lower taxes on the rich, deregulation, privatization of public assets, and declining labor union strength. For their study, the RAND researchers built a simple new metric for measuring how close each income bracket's growth was to the overall GDP, and then looked at what those incomes would be *if* their growth had continued to track GDP. In the real world that we had to live in following the 1980 Reagan Revolution, the growth of the productivity that powers the economy continued, but wages and salaries didn't keep pace.[10] Those diverging variables are the real portrait of neoliberal-ism—a revolution by the rich against the majority, where the work-ing class toil harder and harder but get less and less of the fruit of their labors. Think of all your hours on the clock, *all* that work on those long shifts. It's mostly for the benefit of someone else, usually someone already loaded.

The RAND researchers note that the median US income in 2018 was $36,000, whereas their counterfactual of a continued egalitarian growth regime shows a median income of $57,000. That's a large difference for people, but more hideous is what the counterfactual experiment shows for the richest 1 percent—their yearly income would be $549,000 under the old, more egalitar-ian New Deal system. Not exactly poor. But in reality, the cut-off income of the 1 percent at the time was twice that amount: $1,160,000. RAND, reliant on public funding and not prone to criticizing the system, observed that "those with incomes below the 90th percentile lost a sizable share of their economic power over the last four decades."

But as important as incomes are, they feed into pools of assets known as wealth—while income is a flow, wealth is a stock. For many of us, incomes barely cover costs so our wealth doesn't grow much. The data show the well-to-do have been living a different history indeed.

Classroots

Wealth, defined as assets minus debts, has followed similar growth patterns to those observed in incomes over the modern period. His-torically, wealth overwhelmingly meant land, specifically agricul-turally productive land, often along with various forms of enslaved workers. Wealth reproduced itself but grew only modestly over the long run until the Industrial Revolution, when incomes and wealth rose steeply. This era was the Gilded Age, before the income tax, la-bor unions, and regulations of the later New Deal era. The resulting concentration of wealth during the Gilded Age's heyday was in-credible—historian Steve Fraser observes that "by the midpoint of the Gilded Age . . . the bottom 40 percent came away with 1.1 per-cent."[11] And at the peak of the period in 1910, the richest 1 percent of households owned 45 percent of national wealth and the top 10 percent had a full 80 percent of the pie.[12] By 1929, on the eve of the Great Depression, the 1 percent had gained over half the wealth of the United States.[13]

In the UK, the 1 percent owned an almost unbelievable 70 percent of the national wealth in 1895, and the richest 1/100th of the French owned over half their country then as well.[14] By 1985 the wealth of the richest 1 percent was wrestled down to a low point of only owning a quarter of the nation's wealth in the US, while the top 10 percent held on to 63 percent, somewhat higher than in the European states, which also saw lows of wealth concen-tration at this time.[15] But then came the neoliberal era of Ronald Reagan and Margaret Thatcher across the Western world, the Deng Xiaoping market opening in China, and privatizations worldwide. The results since have been pretty stunning.

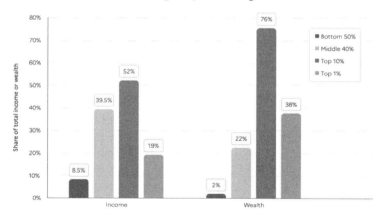

Figure 2. Global income and wealth inequality, 2021. From World Inequality Data-base, https://wid.world/.

For the most recent period of world history, by far the best source of global data on the modern distribution of wealth is the World Inequality Database, which maintains an incredible and up-to-date dataset on who owns what, nationally and globally. Its directors include some of the most recognized economists studying today's drastically lopsided global wealth landscape, including Piketty and the University of California, Berkeley's Emmanuel Saez and Gabriel Zucman. Their website is a stupendous resource for exploring today's ruling class, with excellent data visualization tools, as well as free downloads of their book-length *World Inequality Report*, the last two editions of which I will partly rely on here.[16]

One extremely crucial finding is that over almost forty years, from 1980 to 2017, the 1 percent globally soaked up fully 37 percent of the world's per capita wealth *growth*.[17] This number is an especially rude pie in the face for the many conservative and liberal defenders of capitalism, who insist the way to aid the poor is to increase economic growth. In reality, most of that growth goes to the affluent owners of the giant companies who have great bargaining power in deciding how much corporate income goes to wages for the majority and how much goes to profit for the small stockholding minority. When US president Barack Obama was confronted on cable news with a study finding that 95 *percent* of income gains over his presidency went to the richest 1 percent, he admitted it.[18] Not the kind of change his voters were hoping for.

Incredibly, the WID data from the 1990s to today indicates that global wealth per person grew at an average 3 percent yearly rate for the richest 10 percent of households, 5 percent for the richest 0.1 percent, and indeed "the wealthier the individuals, the higher their increase in wealth . . . The top 0.000001% (one person in 100 million, that is, the top 52 billionaires in 2021) saw their wealth increase by 9.3% per year over the period."[19] The poorest global 50 percent saw their wealth grow at an average annual rate of 3.7 percent, and starting of course from a far, far, far lower point. When economists insist that the best way to help the poor is mainly to support more growth, it should be understood they are promoting a strategy that only further warps the economy and heaps more wealth on people who already have altogether too much.

In the US, these numbers meant rich families took off after 1980, both in dollar terms and in their share of the total national wealth. Despite a lot of claims that today's rich earned their fortunes, the large majority of them are owners of assets like stocks and bonds, not business creators. Their existing wealth makes saving much easier, and the resulting differentials in savings rates "snowballed" into the rich buying more equity at the same time profits rose.[20]

The outcome: by 2021, the richest 1 percent of Americans owned a godforsaken 34.9 percent of our national wealth, with the top 10 percent owning 70.7 percent.[21] Every person who deals with anxiety about paying bills, who is suffering from the inability to pay for medical care, or hoping their oldest kid can hold down the fort while they pick up a shift, should think about the number 34.9 percent every night when falling asleep. The middle class itself, the 40 percent between the bottom half and the top 10 percent, has seen its wealth share fall from 34 percent in 1980 to 28 percent in 2021.[22] So the squeezed middle class is very real, but unfortunately their shrinking economic prospects are leading many of these people to vote for Donald Trump rather than sensible socialists who could actually address their problems (more on which in chapter 7).

An inescapable conclusion is that when millions of people are suffering and dying because of needs they can't afford to address, even though our societies produce goods abundantly, those people are suffering directly for the needless excess affluence of a ruling elite that has absorbed most of the wealth of the former middle class over the last forty years. The WID researchers note that while the US plus Canada are together the richest of the world regions they examine, the region "is also the most unequal when it comes to wealth ownership."[23]

More specifically, Saez and Zucman have published research using Federal Reserve data finding that the top 1 percent in the US had on average $18 million in wealth all told. That works out to *thirty-eight times* the wealth of the average household.[24] So the last forty years of neoliberalism have seen the richest 1 percent's share rise and the bottom 50 percent remain close to zero net wealth, due to its limited assets being matched or exceeded by its debt, especially housing debt. Saez estimates that the richest 1 percent alone gained a full 48 percent of the income growth over the twenty-five years ending in 2018.[25] Authors with *Forbes* found that in 2006 the total wealth of the Forbes 400 was *9.5 percent of US GDP.*[26] Piketty notes, "wealth is so concentrated that a large segment of society is virtually unaware of its existence, so that some people imagine that it belongs to surreal or mysterious entities."[27]

It may be worth noting here that economists widely recognize what we call the "diminishing marginal utility of income," meaning that money does indeed increase personal happiness when people rise from poverty to the middle class, but after that it raises happiness less and less. For example, "Americans who earn $50,000 per year are much happier than those who earn $10,000 per year, but Americans who earn $5 million per year are not much happier than those who earn $100,000 per year."[28] My colleagues are usually shy about drawing the obvious conclusion: that wealth should be redistributed downward from those who won't miss it to those who desperately need relatively modest sums. Economists will come up throughout this book, often in not incredibly flattering ways.

While the rich claim to have earned their huge fortunes through innovation and hard work, inheritance is a giant factor. The dry literature does recognize that "the desire to perpetuate the family fortune has always played a central role," and the schemes by which the wealthy pass their fortunes down to their children is a fascinating subject. In addition to the great inheritance of estates after the death of a senior relative, gifts by living family members have grown significantly in recent decades, mainly to children and often in the form of an investment real estate asset.[29]

Piketty explains, using a mathematical expression that indicates the rate of return, r, on capital exceeds the usual rate of economic growth, g, causing wealth to concentrate:

> Regardless of whether the wealth a person holds at age fifty or sixty is inherited or earned, the fact remains that beyond a certain threshold, capital tends to reproduce itself and accumulates exponentially. The logic of $r > g$ implies that the entrepreneur always tends to turn into a rentier. Even if this happens later in life, the phenomenon becomes important as life expectancy increases. The fact that a person has good ideas at age thirty or forty does not imply that she will still be having them at seventy or eighty, yet her wealth will continue to increase by itself. Or it can be passed on to the next generation and continue to increase there.[30]

The WID researchers also note that wealth has "cumulative effects: for example, it is easier to save if you inherit an apartment and do not have to pay rent."[31]

Luke Savage observed in the socialist magazine *Jacobin* that of the fifty hugely rich families listed on the *Forbes* Billion-Dollar Dynasties list in 2020, more than half were in the Forbes 400 index in 1983.[32] You yourself can keep up with movements of the rich up and down the ranks with the online Bloomberg Billionaires Index.[33] And notably, all the wealth we're talking about here is private, as opposed to public wealth held by governments, like public buildings, treasury balances, and military facilities. The US and most other rich countries have fairly huge amounts of government debt, issued after the country backed away from aggressively taxing the rich over recent decades, enough to make the balance of public wealth close to zero or even negative. This means that private wealth completely dominates the economic profile of society.[34]

These numbers together are approximately a restoration of the levels of inequality of the Gilded Age, of Rockefeller and Carnegie and their monopolies. The scale of that achievement takes some time to really contemplate. The reality of so few individuals and families owning such tremendous oceans of wealth, not just living lives of ludicrous luxury but having so much social importance, is the most central thing—they have so much power over their employees and the government, and the decisions they make, good or bad, have such great consequences for society as a whole. This tremendous economic and social power puts major limitations on the freedom of the rest of us, as we have only a small ability to decide what happens in society, and no positive freedom to consume goods like health care that are produced in huge amounts but only available for those who can pay.[35] Today's resurgent labor movement and Left political leaders, like Bernie Sanders, speak to people's gilded rage.

The Hand That Feeds Them

Some conservatives dispute the stunning numbers produced by the WID and the scholars associated with it. One editorial by two analysts in the *Wall Street Journal*, for example, said the reports "echo a standard left-wing critique of capitalism: Economic growth does not serve all classes of society . . . That portrait of the country is wrong."[36] The editorial then lists several important factors left out of the reports, for example the role played by taxes that pay for transfer payments to poorer parts of society, like food stamps and Medicaid. People's earnings also change over their lifetimes, which snapshot studies omit. And as conservatives often do, the editorial lists all the nice material things, like cell phones, that even poor Americans often have, down to microwave ovens.

Sadly, as with most conservative "rebuttals" to liberal or Left arguments, almost all of it is completely irrelevant. The WID reports, Piketty's major book, Zucman's careful documentation, and many other reports by responsible economists reliably recognize the important role of taxes and transfers, often devoting whole chapters to them. Also, these studies almost always develop distributions of income or wealth over historical time, as we've seen— it's the *opposite* of "snapshot measures." And the fact that poorer echelons of Americans are able to rent apartments with fucking microwave ovens is less impressive than today's think-tank defenders of the rich seem to think. Especially because, as the WID and so many other papers point out, the middle class has sunk deeper into debt since the neoliberal era began in the 1980s—borrowing for those nice homes, borrowing for their increasingly gigantic cars and trucks, and borrowing for their college degrees. The authors of this embarrassing smear piece, Kevin Hassett and Aparna Mathur, are regulars at the *Journal* and hold well-compensated positions at the archconservative, privately funded American Enterprise Institute. It would be more Enterprising of these lazy phonies to read the studies they're pretending to criticize.

Another type of bad argument about the wealth gap comes from liberals of the pro-market type who dominate the political parties that used to be made up of social democrats, like the US Democratic Party or Labour in the UK. Consider Douglas McWilliams, a former IBM economist and corporate consultant, who's critical of this whole body of research in his own book on inequality, *The Inequality Paradox*. Unfortunately, the only research he ever refers to is Piketty's breakout hit book, and like many reviewers he appears not to have read the long text. He calls the entire approach a "conspiracy theory" based on Marxist concepts of exploitation.[37]

In fact, Piketty's book mostly pins inequality on an empirical mathematical relationship, $r > g$, which suggests capital accumulates more quickly than the broader economy grows, driving up inequality over time. Most of the big shifts are attributed to major social changes like industrialization and the New Deal, which are pretty far from secret conspiracies. McWilliams shows his cards when he says he's "on the side of reducing poverty, which seems to me to be more important than reducing inequality." This fails to recognize the incredible power that huge fortunes put in the hands of the rich, by whom he's employed after all. Worse, like other liberals and conservatives he argues the best way to reduce poverty is to increase economic growth, but as we've already seen, a cartoonishly lopsided majority of today's economic growth flows into the already very richest pockets. He goes on to actually suggest that people documenting inequality really just resent not being able to afford the expensive London neighborhood he lives in.[38]

A further embarrassment for more conservative economists like these is that the facts are backed up by other researchers who are far less critical of the current system, including those at the Federal Reserve. The Fed is America's central bank, with a number of roles including organizing the big bailout packages we need for our giant banking corporations every few years, as well as running monetary policy, where interest rates are adjusted up or down to slow or speed up the economy. The Fed's policymakers are mostly bankers and financial experts from Wall Street and around the US, but the system produces a very rich output of economic research.

One useful class of public data the Fed maintains is the DFA, the Distributional Financial Accounts.[39] These are quarterly estimates of the amounts and different forms of wealth in the US, using data from the highly reputable Survey of Consumer Finances and the Financial Accounts of the United States, huge datasets maintained by the Fed's regular surveys of households. While only extending the last thirty-odd years, they still capture a great deal of information about the evolution of incomes, wealth, debt, and many other fascinating variables. The most recent data presently available, for the third quarter 2021, has the richest 1 percent owning 32.1 percent of all wealth, and the top 10 percent owning 69.6 percent. It's pretty close to the WID's numbers, and the point is that all serious research agrees that the richest households have a hugely disproportionate share of economic resources, and crucially that nearly all the economic *growth* of the last several decades has gone to these richest echelons. Indeed, the pyramiding of income and wealth at the top of the distribution is one of the better-proven conclusions in today's social sciences. The Fed's data are download-able and also packed with visualization tools.

The pandemic years only threw fuel on this raging fire. When the COVID-19 shutdowns took effect in early 2020, it played to the business models of the Big Tech platform corporations like Google, Amazon, and Facebook (now Meta). The tech companies' stocks exploded as earnings skyrocketed, enriching the ruling class, which owns most stock (see below), but especially the bil-lionaire founders of those companies. From March 2020 to March 2021, Jeff Bezos's fortune grew by a staggering $58 billion; Google cofounders Sergey Brin and Larry Page were enriched by $32 and $33 billion, respectively; and Facebook's Mark Zuckerberg gained $29 billion while his platform played a major role spreading mis-information about COVID that likely worsened the plague.[40] In total, the collective wealth of all America's billionaires rose from $2.95 trillion at the start of the pandemic to $4.56 trillion a year later.[41] Incredible.

For the majority of us, of course, rising mortgage, credit card, and student debts took off in the 1980s when wages started stag-nating, and these debts count against wealth. Total household debt was 75 percent of national income in the mid-1980s, reached 135 percent in 2009 after the financial crisis, and stood at 110 percent in 2012. So over this whole period "the bottom half of the distri-bution always owns close to zero net wealth," the WID research-ers note, "when including negative wealth such as credit card and housing debt."[42]

The Harvard Business-Duke survey study mentioned above is important to keep in mind when considering these numbers. Recall that a surprisingly large consensus in the random survey sample, including even wealthier households and conservatives, preferred a distribution of wealth closer to the social democratic Scandina-vian model, where the top 10 percent own a mere 32 percent of the wealth.[43] A staggering *92 percent* said they preferred that setup to a distribution typical of the US. Meanwhile the survey participants estimated on average that in the US the richest 20 percent owns 59 percent of the total national wealth, whereas the real number at the time was about 84 percent.

And importantly, this level of concentration of wealth is present in the US across demographic groups, including the most frequently discussed ones of race, education, and age. Discussion in America of economic inequality is often in terms of differences among these groups in the US, due to its long history of racism, the earnings premium of education, and the fact that people save over their life spans and tend to be richer later in life than earlier.

But writer and policy developer Matt Bruenig analyzed the Fed's Survey of Consumer Finances for the socialist magazine *Jacobin* and found that "in reality, the level of wealth inequality within each group is virtually identical to the wealth inequality that we see in the society as a whole."[44] In other words, among white families, Black families, those holding a college degree, those without a degree, and regardless of age group, the top 10 percent owned 69 percent to 74 percent of the total wealth *of that demographic group.* Using SCF data, Bruenig presents the distribution of wealth owned by each 10 percent of households, for white families, Hispanic, and Black, for those without a high school degree, those with college degrees, those with head of household aged eighteen to thirty-five, those thirty-six to fifty, and they are all nearly identical. Huge numbers for the top tenth regardless of their demographic characteristics, a smaller share for the next 10 percent, and crumbs for the rest. Bruenig notes that the difference in wealth between the average US white and Black family is $160,710. That's a lot of money, but "the $181,440 net worth of the median white family is less than one-fourth of the $746,821 they would have if all the country's wealth were distributed evenly."

All the Money in the World

Outside the US, the wealth landscape isn't much better. To be a part of the global 1 percent, you need just under $3 million in assets, a threshold met by families making up fifty-one million people worldwide. Across all countries, the richest one in a hundred families owns 38 percent of the stupendous $557 trillion of global wealth.[45] The richest 10 percent own a towering 76 percent of global wealth, while the bottom half of the world's population has about 2 percent of the total. Different regions of the world vary, as we'll see, but in a limited range shaped by modern global capitalism: the top tenth always owns between 60 and 80 percent of regional wealth, and the bottom half is almost always under 5 percent.[46]

In Europe, their top 1 percent of households has had a striking recovery from the high-tax era of postwar social democracy, although not as stunning as in the US. Britain's 1 percent, for example, owned 70 percent of the nation's wealth in 1914; today it makes do with only around 20 to 22 percent.[47] Conspicuously, Europe is one of the few regions where the austerity policies wreaking havoc around the world have been less effective. National health and education systems have resisted the budget cuts and privatizations of the last forty years, and as a result, it's the only region where the middle-class 40 percent still has more income than the top 10 percent.[48] Nowhere else is this true today.

China is still ruled by its Communist Party, but since its opening to private investment and privatizations it has gained the capitalist features of fast economic growth and a hyper-rich owning class. China's richest 1 percent today owns 30.5 percent of the nation's wealth, and the top 10 percent owns 67.8 percent.[49] An enormous number of people in China have been lifted out of global poverty due to the country's state-led market development model, with the country's own bottom 50 percent holding 6.5 percent of national wealth, very low but a relatively rich share by world standards. China's inequality has increased using more limited measures as well, including the traditional Gini coefficient.[50]

Across the world more broadly, the pattern continues and the difference is especially steep for the large realms of the world known as the developing world, or formerly the "Third World," including the regions of Latin America, South Asia, and Africa—showing the long legacy of European colonialism and high debt levels since then. India and China both had large industrial sectors in their economies for centuries, and as late as 1800, the two together made up over half of world manufacturing output at 53 percent. By 1900, after the brutal British colonization of India and the partitioning of Ming China into captive spheres of influences by all the European powers plus Japan, their share was just 5 percent. The WID researchers note that the share of world income going to the poorest 50 percent of the world's people, who are almost entirely in the developing world, is still today about *half* what it was in 1820 at the dawn of the colonial era.[51] Just a blessing for the struggling masses, colonialism.

And indeed, despite the world's poor being mostly in the developing world, billions of dollars a year in interest payments are paid by the Third World to lenders in London, New York, and Paris. While the poor countries today are no longer under the formal control of the rich countries, they do still send a heavy flow of assets to them, due to debts run up by dictators, and from the rich of the Western countries buying up assets in the poor ones during upheavals and recessions. This hideously perverted flow of money from the poor to the rich continues to this day, and the poorest countries on Earth still owe literal trillions to wealthy bondholders in rich countries that ruled them for centuries and stripped them of their wealth (see chapter 6).[52]

Of course, the forms that all this wealth takes vary widely, within countries and especially between them. The rich of all countries own huge fortunes in financial assets, multiple residences, and other high-end real estate. Many also own mineral deposits, oil and gas rights, legal licenses to valuable intellectual property, bank accounts with big electronic balances, and, of course, good old-fashioned cash. The history of each region and country makes a huge difference for the local ruling class profile. The richest families in South Africa and many of the former Latin American colonial possessions have unusually white complexions, often being descended from a local Europeanized elite or big white colonial landholders. America and Europe's numbers show you don't have to be an imperial possession of another country for centuries to have an awful tiny ruling class, but in the former colonies, which contain most of the world's population today, the people in charge are often descendants and inheritors of colonial exploiters and slave owners.

So no matter how poor the country today, it has a tiny elite with wealth similar to that of the richest families in the developed countries. In the developed world, the richest 1 percent of households owns 25 percent of all wealth in Europe, 30 percent in East Asia, and 35 percent in North America; and in the developing world, the richest one-hundredth owns 46 percent of all wealth in Latin America and in Russia, 38 percent in Sub-Saharan Africa, 30 percent in India, and 44 percent in the Middle East.[53] The WID website has data for most countries broken down to various scales, so anyone can find out precisely how hard their country is getting screwed by capitalism.

But having reviewed all these figures for today's hyperconcentration of wealth, it's important to recognize that wealth comes with *power*, and combined with the power of the state wielded by political figures, it's the source of the influence and control of the ruling class. Power is not only about the state, and its institutions of the legislature and courts and police and military, although God knows they're crucial. Power comes in various forms, legal and military but also economic and ideological.

Some forms of wealth make this especially clear. Piketty estimates that by the start of the US Civil War, the four million slaves in the South had a total market value equal to about a year and a half of the national US income, "roughly equal to the total value of farmland."[54] The point very definitely still holds today. If you're a power-hungry megalomaniac, you can seek authority by running for a government position or working up to a senior position in a public bureaucracy or the military, gaining very real but legally limited power. Alternatively, you could build a business that makes you rich without any limit, and push your employees around and drug test them and make them listen to awful music while they work all day. You can buy a media empire and shape the ideas that everyone hears and thinks about day after day. With a ton of money you can invest in things you want and lobby the government to prevent things you don't.

Money and economic control mean power, and that's the heart of the ruling class. And the very best place to see that is the intersection of the world's rich and the corporate empires they own.

Lock, Stock, and Barrel

Big fortunes aren't held in cash. The towering wealth of the really rich certainly includes generous demand deposits, but the hallmark of a rich family is its well-diversified investment portfolio, including asset classes like government bonds, real estate, and financial securities. Above all, these financial assets include corporate stock— pieces of ownership of companies. If you buy corporate stock, or "equities," you own a bit of the firm and are entitled to a proportional piece of its profit. Companies issue these shares when they "go public," inviting investors to buy into a growing business and own a piece of its profitability.

Big corporations often have many millions of shares outstanding, reflecting decades of expansion and many rounds of cash-raising. This means investors only sometimes exercise any direct control over the companies they own, although there are important exceptions and large stockholders can generally get a hearing with senior executives or get seats on corporate boards. Stanley Aronowitz noted in his book *How Class Works* that CEOs serve the shareholders—which they are themselves, due to their stock-heavy pay package. He wrote, "We have seen how vulnerable top executives are, as boards of directors dismiss them after a few quarters of low profitability."[55] Ownership of large amounts of stock in the gigantic corporations that dominate our market system, from Wall Street to Silicon Valley, means ownership of the productive economy. And this form of wealth, riskier than others but with potentially much higher yields, is even more concentrated than the rest of wealth.

The definitive work on US stock ownership is by economist Edward Wolff, of New York University and the National Bureau of Economic Research. In a series of research papers, Wolff confronted the idea of the "shareholder democracy," popular among liberals and conservatives, which claims that because many US households own stock, most Americans benefit from rising corporate profits and a booming stock market. But Wolff discovered that, in fact, the proportion of Americans owning any stock peaked at 51.9 percent in 2001, fell in recession, recovered between market crashes, and then plunged again to 46.9 percent after the 2008 finance crisis.[56] So the first point is that not even a bare majority of US households own any stock at all.

But the far greater point is that in addition to this limited participation, "many of these families had only a minor stake in the stock market in 2010, with only 34% with total stock holdings worth $5,000 (in 1995 dollars) or more ... and only 22% with holdings worth $25,000 or more."[57] Middle-class wealth is mostly tied up in physical assets, primarily the personal home along with cars and other personal property. Wolff found the middle swath of American households has three-fifths of their assets invested in their homes, although due to large mortgage debt, housing wealth is limited even among the middle class. In contrast, the richest 20 percent of Americans own their main home outright almost universally, and often have other real estate.

The bottom line is that stock ownership is "highly skewed by wealth class. The top one percent of households classified by wealth owned 40 percent of all stocks in 2016, and the top 10 percent 84 percent, and the top quintile 93 percent."[58] Other business assets are even more concentrated.[59] And notably, "there are striking differences in returns by wealth class. The returns on gross assets were generally higher for the top 1% than for the middle three quintiles . . . The differences reflect the greater share of high yield investment assets like stocks in the portfolios of the rich and the greater share of housing in the portfolio of the middle class."[60]

Piketty's meticulous analysis of modern wealth data also found "the importance of real estate decreases sharply as one moves higher in the wealth hierarchy. In the '9 percent' group . . . real estate accounts for half of total wealth . . . In the top centile, by contrast, financial and business assets clearly predominate over real estate. In particular, shares of stock or partnerships constitute nearly the totality of the largest fortunes . . . Housing is the favorite investment of the middle class and moderately well-to-do, but true wealth always consists primarily of financial and business assets."[61]

As the socialist economics magazine *Dollars & Sense* put it, "Americans are treated to a daily stock market report on the nightly news. And for some (a small minority) this report will have considerable relevance. But for the vast majority of viewers, the numbers will seem unconnected to their daily struggle to make ends meet—because they are."[62] Even the *New York Times* recognized that "riotous market swings . . . have virtually no impact on the income or wealth of most families. The reason: They own little or no stock. . . Roughly half of all households don't have a cent invested in stocks, whether through a 401(k) account or shares in General Electric."[63]

This also means, of course, that they sit out the stock market rallies, which recently brought the richest 10 percent to owning a new high of 88.8 percent of outstanding stock in 2021, according to the Fed's DFA data.[64] That's an especially big deal in this

neoliberal era of gigantic global corporations, often monopolies or
at least oligopolies, because profits are so tremendously high after
decades of mergers and outsourcing. The high inflation following
the COVID-19 pandemic gave many large, consolidated firms an
opportunity to raise prices faster than costs and widen their profit
margins further.[65]

Corporations return money to their stockholders either by
issuing a share of profits to them, called dividends, or by buying up
their own stock, which tends to increase its price and thus increase
shareholder wealth. The business press reports that after pausing
these payouts during the uncertainty of the pandemic, companies
paid out $20.3 billion in dividends and spent over $500 billion on
buybacks in just the first half of 2021.[66] By 2023 they were projected to clear $1 trillion.[67] This is where the wealth of society is
located, and since publicly traded corporations are owned by rich
households across the land, C. Wright Mills memorably wrote in
The Power Elite that the corporate world "is, in operating fact, class-
wide property."[68]

Beyond just having piles of cash and fancy personal property,
it is this that defines the real modern ruling class—ownership of
the productive economy. This extremely high level of centralization
of business equity means that despite fashionable claims that the
ruling class is made up of sleek professionals in media or influencer
roles, the real ruling class is an *owning* class that not only possesses
vast liquid wealth but owns most of the world of big business.
When stock markets boom, as they have for the last few decades
(between dizzying crashes), and companies report years of gigantic record-breaking profits, you may benefit a bit if you hold some
shares or have a decent retirement account. But the world of big
business is mainly the property of the richest households, and this
nexus of corporate power and rich families should be a central part
of anyone's understanding of who's really in charge of the world.

For the ruling class, a share is a thing you own, not a thing
you do.

And the same hyperconcentration of financial assets is present in more cutting-edge markets like cryptocurrencies, the new electronic assets that claim to be potentially usable as decentralized money systems, outside the control of governments and banks. The National Bureau of Economic Research recently found that about 0.01 percent of the holders of Bitcoin, the most popular cryptocurrency, own 27 percent of the existing nineteen million Bitcoin. The conservative *Wall Street Journal* laughed that for all its hype of decentralization, "the top bitcoin holders control a greater share of the cryptocurrency than the most affluent American households control in dollars."[69]

This relatively brief survey of the scale of the owning class's wealth hoard is enough to paint the picture. Since the world elite turned against social democracy in the 1980s and '90s, the already-rich were swamped with a tsunami of wealth as their taxes fell and their stocks rallied. From cash to equities to fancy toys, the economic growth that capitalism is so famous for has piled up in the portfolios of the very very richest people and their insufferable families. The amount of money involved is sometimes really beyond the ability of the person on the street to easily understand— the worker who spends long shifts toiling for $9 an hour has a tough time picturing what a billion-dollar lifestyle really looks like.

So what *does* it look like? Even as their fortunes grow, the ruling class spends a monumentally warped amount of money on just the craziest tacky crap you ever heard of, from fancy clothes to personal staff to giant vacation homes to metaverse NFTs. Their catered-to coked-up pampered-ass lifestyle is the subject of the next chapter.

CHAPTER 2

THE LIFESTYLE

IT'S WORSE THAN YOU THINK

Well, I do think it's excessive . . . It is absolutely excessive. No question about it. But it's amazing what you can get used to.
—**Larry Ellison, on his megayacht**[1]

First launched in 1943 as a Canadian warship, [the yacht Christina O] was present at the Normandy landings before being purchased by Greek shipping magnate Aristotle Onassis and beginning her life as a pleasure cruiser. Elizabeth Taylor and Frank Sinatra sipped cocktails on the boat's whale-foreskin bar stools.
— **Rory Satran, "What the World's Richest People Wear on Yachts"**[2]

P rivate luxury jets. Spacious elite penthouses towering over major global cities. Enormous pleasure yachts made with forty million worker-hours. Food literally dusted with gold. A safe full of visas and foreign passports. Huge closets full of stunningly expensive high-end clothes. Private chefs in your private suite at a private resort. Million-dollar watches. An entourage of ass-kissing sycophants.

Now that we've seen the stupendous amount of cash, equity, and assets in the vaults and portfolios of the ruling class, the inevitable question is, where does it all go? Middle-class people sometimes imagine that the rich only fly first class and send their kids to the best schools in town. In fact, the really rich fly on their private aircraft (making enormous additions to our environmental crisis) and raise their kids with private tutors, followed by hyper-elite academies with tiny class sizes, while personal staff do their errands and chores.

It all flows into the endless river of utter wasted excess that decorates the days of the ruling class. The $100 million estates, the cosmetic surgery, the acres of classic paintings kept in storage units in Switzerland, and their family names on universities and public parks. There is no limit to the bottomless depravity and naked egomania of the highest-wealth households.

The Fun Percent

The universally recognized founding text for understanding the consumption spending of the rich is *The Theory of the Leisure Class*, by the Norwegian-American sociologist Thorstein Veblen. The 1899 book is the origin of the term "conspicuous consumption"—the concept that expensive goods and services are consumed partially just to impress peers, and of course people of lesser means. Beyond clear enrichment and "the power conferred by wealth," Veblen held there is the desire to establish oneself as a great figure: "In order to gain and to hold the esteem of men it is not sufficient merely to possess wealth or power. The wealth or power must be put in evidence, for esteem is awarded only on evidence. And not only does the evidence of wealth serve to impress one's importance on others . . . but it is of scarcely less use in building up and preserving one's self-complacency."[3]

Referring especially to classic centers of wealth like noble households but also today's more established rich families, Veblen found "refined tastes, manners, and habits of life are a useful evidence of gentility, because good breeding requires time, application, and expense, and can therefore not be compassed by those whose time and energy are taken up with work . . . In the last analysis the value of manners lies in the fact that they are the voucher of a life of leisure."[4]

When you have still more wealth to show off and even richer jerk friends to compete with, you can get staffed beyond your needs, with more of "those servants who are in most immediate and obvious attendance upon their master. So that the utility of these comes to consist in great part, in their conspicuous exemption from productive labour and in the evidence which this exemption affords of their master's wealth and power," which Veblen somewhat amusingly calls "vicarious leisure."[5]

Peter Bearman's fascinating book *Doormen*, on the professionals who monitor the front doors at high-end city buildings, observes that doormen sometimes "see themselves solely as conspicuous display items for the tenants to consume." One is quoted saying, "Some people will stand there in the cold just 'cause they don't want to open the door. It's funny how the wealthier side is living 'cause you know it's kind of weird . . . Sometimes they'll even ring the doorbell, and they'll just wait. All they have to do is open it, but sometimes I'm like on the intercom or working the elevators but they'll still stay there. It's like they're frozen or something."[6]

But high-end consumption—whether to wow the average Joe on the street, your fellow rotten elite friends, or yourself—has grown with the wealth of the ruling class. Let me take you on a tour, first with an item from the *Wall Street Journal*.

An elegant stone façade just off the Champs Élysées hides what may be the world's most elite liquor store. Spirits maker Moët Hennessy has turned a Parisian apartment into a discreet, invitation-only boutique for its best clients and those of its parent, luxury giant LVMH Moët Hennessy

Louis Vuitton. Decades-old bottles of limited edition Dom Pérignon champagne, costing thousands of dollars each, lie in a temperature-controlled closet made of crystal glass. A display case holds massive 'Nebuchadnezzar' bottles of Cheval Blanc, each containing almost four gallons of the ultraexpensive Saint-Émilion wine. The apartment, opened a year ago, is part of an intensifying effort by luxury firms to pamper their best-heeled customers . . . The clientele isn't the 1% of the world's richest people. It is the top 0.1%, a group that already makes up a disproportionate percentage of sales for the industry, which corresponds to Ultra-High Net Worth Individuals, the roughly 211,000 people around the world with individual net worth of more than $30 million.[7]

The *Journal* continues: "High-end menswear firm Stefano Ricci flies its tailors to clients around the world to make custom suits. Each suit costs between $10,000 and $20,000, and customers are expected to purchase at least five for a tailor to make the trip . . . The Ricci family recently opened a country house near its headquarters in Florence where it hosts top-spending clients, even allowing them to drive the family's collection of vintage cars."

Regrettably, however, there's a common lament in high-end commerce: "Why the Rich Are Bad Customers," as the business press puts it. A top executive at Barclays Wealth said rich clients make "demanding and often unreasonable requests" and "impossible demands on an organization." Very high-end clients, those in the $100 million territory, demand institutional pricing—the reduced-price volume discounts given to large companies or governments. A billionaire gloats, "The best part about being rich is all the free stuff you can demand."[8]

But money talks. When hedge fund tyrant and Trump adviser Stephen Schwarzman turned sixty in 2007, he hired the enormous Park Avenue armory and turned it into, for real, "a large-scale replica of the Schwarzmans' Manhattan apartment," as the *New Yorker* famously reported. "Replicas of Schwarzman's art collection were mounted on the walls, including, at one entrance, a full-length portrait of him by Andrew Festing, the president of the Royal Society of Portrait Painters. Dinner was served in a faux night-club setting, with orchids and palm trees. Guests dined on lobster, filet mignon, and baked Alaska, and were offered an array of expensive wines."[9] Martin Short emceed, Patti LaBelle and Rod Stewart sang. Guests included the chairman of Sony, New York cardinal Edward Egan, and the governor of the State of New York.[10] Eighteen months later the financial world was in flames and Schwarzman was far richer.

Not having attracted enough infamy at his sixtieth, when Schwarzman turned seventy he threw himself another over-the-top affair, with a sea of valets, servers, bartenders, live camels, trapeze artists, Mongolian soldiers, and drivers. Gwen Stefani sang "Happy Birthday" to a guest list including senior Wall Street grandees from brand-name firms like Carlyle, Barclays, Citigroup, and KKR, billionaire industrialist David Koch, and Trump treasury secretary Wilbur Ross. The president himself did not appear, although Schwarzman served on a Trump administration advisory council, and Trump's kids Ivanka and Jared Kushner did make it.

Also among the guests was David Boaz, a VP at the Cato Institute, the prominent libertarian think tank. Boaz apparently was present mainly to ensure that a furious public would get plenty of capitalist propaganda in the coverage this time around: "It's not as if he hasn't been generous . . . It's his money. He can do whatever he wants with it . . . He earned it."[11] Schwarzman's birthday boots must have had a lustrous shine indeed!

Schwarzman may be the modern leader of conspicuous consumption, but his Wall Street brethren blazed the trail. Financiers led the still-popular trend among the world's rich of literally *eating gold*, shaved or sprinkled as a topping onto cake, cappuccinos, and champagne, according to the *Journal*'s reporting with the frank headline "Why the Rich Like to Eat Gold."[12] This was right after the 2008 finance disaster, so presumably the reason is "because they are detached spoiled-rich princelings sulking from their public scoldings." For some, merely eating it isn't enough. Robert Frank includes in his book *Richistan* an anecdote of a Florida old-money gentleman who owns a solid-gold straw for sipping champagne.[13]

It's a pattern as old as American capitalism. A famous 1897 costume ball at the Waldorf in New York saw the rich host appearing as Louis XIV, the Sun King himself, and fifty, *fifty*, women who came dressed as Marie Antoinette. The party was also arguably slightly insensitive since a depression had begun four years earlier.[14]

The socialist writer Nathan Robinson read a stack of books by billionaires (or their hired ghostwriters) and quotes Ken Langone, CEO of Home Depot, who wrote in his memoir: "Should I follow the Bible? I'll be honest: I'm not giving everything away. Why? Because I love this life! I love having nice houses and good people to help me. I love getting on my airplane instead of having to take my shoes off and wait in line to take a commercial flight. You want to accuse me of living well? I plead guilty . . . As I said, I've been rich and I've been poor, and rich is better."[15]

Inconspicuous Consumption

Even in Veblen's time he recognized the rich were becoming somewhat more demure than their wild ruling-class party era of the Gilded Age, partially due to rising public resentment and growing labor and socialist movements. Especially since the New Deal era of the 1930s to 1970s, when an organized labor movement led a democratic drive to tax the rich and break up their corporate monopolies, many of the rich have been wary of flaunting it *too* much. This sadly short-lived history has led to a pretty hilarious persecution complex among certain billionaires who, despite owning a large chunk of society and being quite able to get their views out by buying TV networks or state senators, whine nonstop to their journalist employees about their surviving taxes and regulations. Ex–Starbucks CEO Howard Schultz said even the term "billionaire" had become unfair and that "people of wealth" would be better.[16] Many "people of wealth" are still excited to throw big parties and plaster their names on stadiums and giant publicly visible mansions, but others prefer anonymity and don't put themselves out—beyond maybe placing their name on a large university campus building they paid for.[17]

Rather than give up the parties, today the rich are instead frequently less conspicuous in their personal affectations. You may have noticed that cartoons depicting rich people often show them in very dated attire—monocles and top hats. This was the ruling-class-signifying attire of the Gilded Age in the late nineteenth and early twentieth centuries, and since then the rich have sadly learned to tone it down. The preference for clothes among the rich is now often a T-shirt and blue jeans public-facing persona, even if the actual T-shirt and jeans of that dressed-down look are insanely costly.

The writer and architecture critic Kate Wagner wrote for the *Nation* that "You Can't Even Tell Who's Rich Anymore," finding "One of the great disappointments of contemporary life is that in times of hopelessly vast income inequality, society's arch-capitalists . . . are boring. The zenith of their boringness? How they dress."[18] She notes Facebook CEO Mark Zuckerberg wearing Patagonia vests with a pullover, Bill Gates's khakis and loafers, and the endless tech guys in "an ill-fitting blazer with a T-shirt and jeans." She mentions Alexandre Arnault of LVMH, who "does not know how to wear clothes. He only knows how to lard his frail, millionaire body with various hype-driven status symbols . . . You used to be able to look at someone and tell that they were rich. Clothes have always been an important class signifier." But now the styles of the rich "are often borrowed or stolen from the lower classes by the upper. The heirs of old wealth go to private colleges and wear the same Carhartt jackets owned by truck drivers. Tech billionaires try to look like your neighbors or pensioners." Veblen said it was "seldom altogether unaffected . . . that make-believe of rusticity."[19]

Paul Fussell's popular book *Class* refers to the richest households as being "top-out-of-sight," since their gigantic wealth is now often hidden behind closed gates. "Showing off used to be the main satisfaction of being very rich in America," he wrote. "Now the rich must skulk and hide. It's a pity."[20] But Fussell wrote at the very start of neoliberalism in the early 1980s, when the New Deal–era wary watchfulness of the rich still lingered. Today, while the rich like to publicly project a dressed-down aesthetic, we can learn from *Forbes* journalists in their book *All the Money in the World* how the money gets privately spent in a typical rich-person-year, including loafers for $410, dress shoes for $4,000, $40,000 for prep school, $7,600 for caviar, $8,000 for fresh flower arrangements for six rooms in season, $14,000 for a facelift, $1,300 for a day in concierge hospital care, $4.8 million for a yacht, $1.3 million for an Olympic-size pool, $8 million for a private plane, $11 million for a private helicopter.[21] Or cough up a couple hundred million to buy a beloved sports team and then move it across the country.[22]

But the wealthy across eras do have a well-known history of cosplaying as the normal classes. John Kampfner's incredible historical survey *The Rich* describes how "millionaire coal mine owners gave dinners with their servants dressed as miners. One event was themed the 'poverty social,' where guests came dressed in rags and 'scraps of food were served on wooden plates. The diners sat about on broken soapboxes, buckets and coal hods. Newspapers, dust cloths and old skirts were used as napkins, and beer served in a rusty tin can.'"[23]

In his book on the 1 percent, author Paul Street wrote, "Another factor contributing to the relatively invisible and 'unseeable' nature of the wealthy 'true elite' is the reluctance of many rich people to flaunt their wealth and the determination of many elites to cloak that wealth in more plebian or at least middle-class wrappings . . . [C]onspicuous consumption went 'underground.'" Now "the 1% prefers on the whole to keep its opulence behind private walls and gates, making it less likely to provoke popular ire in the supposed 'land of equality.'"[24]

Some forms of consumption remain inherently conspicuous, like that popular pastime of the ruling and even middle classes—cosmetic surgery. While a mass-market product, high-end services are stunningly costly and elite. Steven Gaines's book on South Beach high society describes Dr. Leonard Roudner, known as the "breast man" in Miami, charging $7,000 a pair. "He was so busy that he operated on five women every day of the week and squeezed in two more implants every other Saturday . . . He'd even shaped the breasts of three generations of women in the same family."[25]

If there is one term reliably used when marketing to the rich, it is "exclusive." Exclusive destinations, exclusive service, exclusive accommodations. Exclusive here of course means it is prohibitively expensive for the typical person, and therefore suggests only a certain type of people are let in, excluding the riff raff. It's fascinating, because society at large has been struggling for years with trying to become more *inclusive*, especially since the racial unrest of 2020. There's been some real effort for more inclusive institutions, media images, and especially language, in terms of race and gender. Many conservatives, who are mainly animated politically to defend traditional hierarchies in society, are furious about these "woke" developments, but for societies as cruelly racially discriminatory as the US and many other modern states, it's hard not to view it as a broadly positive development.

Which makes it interesting that we have a remaining form of very open exclusivity right in plain view in our society, *class-based* exclusion, in addition to the perhaps better-recognized forms of racial exclusion. The ubiquitous, and I mean ubiquitous, use of the word "exclusive" in marketing to rich consumers shows it, especially in pitches to the UHNWIs, as marketing literature calls people with over $30 million American.

Consider watches. The industry had its best year ever in 2021, by selling less. "The Swiss watch industry is moving ever further upmarket as brand owners target rich consumers and try to differentiate their products from the Apple Watch and other wearable tech."[26] High-end Rolex units start at $10,000 and the sky's the limit. Some super-high-end units sell for a million bucks. The business press notes some smaller more down-market watchmakers charge just a few grand, "offering an 'inclusive' form of luxury to which most consumers can realistically aspire."

Apple itself is definitely the higher end of the mobile electronics marketplace but is seen as representing middle-class affluence, rather than a maker of actual elite goods. This is important to the marketing of the Apple brand and its access to broad middle-class markets globally, although it does flirt with more exclusivity, as in 2015 when it released the Apple Watch Hermès, having a specially styled interface, the first tie-in for the company with a luxury brand. The special edition watch cost $1,500, but the company's famous former design chief, Jonathan Ive, "resists the notion that Apple is becoming exclusive, a defining characteristic of luxury goods."[27]

And when Bill Gates's ex-wife and billion-dollar charity co-kingpin, Melinda French, traveled to Manhattan to appear on NBC's *Today* show, she was preceded by a "military operation"–level security detail, on the scale of a visiting foreign dignitary. This personal army of security consultants did a sweep of the full studio prior to her arrival, with sources at the show saying even Beyoncé and Michelle Obama didn't have such an expansive security apparatus. French was appearing to promote her new book imprint about authors striving for "radical inclusion."[28] Unfortunately this required excluding everyone else from the area.

Haute Divorce

All relationships age and some don't age well. In the modern world, separation and divorce allow unhappy marriages to be dissolved—a mercy to the couple and sometimes their kids. But when you have billions of dollars of various kinds of assets, things have a way of getting messier, as recent divorces at the very, very high end of the wealth distribution have shown. Of course, in cases of separation it's far better for the kids when their parents settle amicably, where the parties agree or use arbitration to split assets in a civil manner. But for a ruling class–analyzing creep like me, ugly, contentious divorces are way better, since those go to court and some court records get publicly released, which is great for books like this.

The *New York Times*, for example, reports on "a 1 Percent Divorce" between two heinous New York real estate assholes. The marriage fell apart with the 2008 crash, leading to the unhappy couple suing one another over things like $12 million in artwork, $1.8 million in jewelry, and "a pair of Albert Cheuret sconces, circa 1925, which were valued at $100,000."[29] But they come much, much bigger. The Bezoses', for example, although they settled amicably.

But the really big one is the Gateses'. With one of history's great fortunes, estimated at $124 billion at the time of the filing, this process will go on for years. Assets include a stock portfolio with billions in diversified equities, a large stake in the Four Seasons luxury hotel chain, various mansions in Washington and California, huge tracts of land that formerly made Gates the biggest single private owner of farmland in the US, a stake in a company serving private jet owners, and one of Leonardo da Vinci's notebooks. For all the stupendous extent of the assets, "lawyers point out that the issues that cause friction in the average divorce are completely absent for the stratospherically wealthy," as middle-class couples may find themselves comfortable, but not wealthy enough to be comfortable once everything is split in half.[30] Much of this great wealth is hidden secretively behind shell companies with purposefully boring, generic names. And of course this is all before even talking about the Bill & Melinda Gates Foundation and its $50 billion endowment, which is in a trust that can't be divided in the marital estate, so it should remain intact to needlessly dominate the world of philanthropy for years to come (see chapter 4).

Uglier cases occur, as with the Bosarges. Wilbur Bosarge got rich quick through high-frequency trading and took his wife Marie on a spending spree on art, antiques, three yachts, and thirteen homes. But when the octogenarian billionaire left his wife for his twentysomething Russian mistress, the result was "A High-Stakes Divorce Illustrates How the Rich Play Real-Estate Tug of War," as the *Journal* headline read. The former Mrs. Bosarge soon discovered she had no access to any of their 13 homes, or their private island in the Bahamas, because "the Bosarges—like many ultrawealthy people across the globe—own their homes through a complex network of trusts and limited liability companies. Now that they are divorcing, Mrs. Bosarge said her husband is using these complex ownership structures . . . to essentially eliminate her stake in the homes, and to prevent her from accessing what she said is billions in cash and other property."[31] The extremely complex details arise from the US state South Dakota wildly loosening its laws around trusts, allowing trust holders to domicile property from around the world, to hold it with near-complete anonymity, and to even alter the trust terms without notification of those named in the trust. The former Mrs. Bosarge may therefore fail to collect money even if victorious in divorce court.

Then there's the kids. Elite youth attend Financial Life Skills retreats, studying portfolio theory, debt management, and prenups, and above all learning "how *not* to squander their fortunes." The issue is serious, as surveys of rich families find almost 40 percent of millionaires give their children unrestricted access to the kids' money, rather than putting any brakes on it. Further, wealth research firms find "most millionaires today plan to leave at least 75 percent of their estates to their children. The number is highest for families with households worth $25 million or more, disproving the widely held notion that wealthier families are more likely to leave a greater share to charity."[32]

It can go well—consider LVMH, the great European luxury conglomerate mentioned earlier, run by Bernard Arnault, one of the megabillionaires who trades world's-richest-man status with Bill Gates, Jeff Bezos, and Elon Musk. The business press recently ran a long article, "The World's Richest Person Auditions His Five Children to Run LVMH, the Luxury Empire," and it's exactly what it sounds like. Arnault is grooming his adult kids to run various branches of the sprawling firm, even having them weigh in on managers, and they share voting power on the holding company that owns the conglomerate. When inflation rose steeply in 2022 and public resentment mounted with it, Arnault's oldest son "suggested LVMH launch an ad campaign publicizing how much the company paid in French taxes last year and the number of jobs it created . . . His father took the advice."[33]

Finally, before moving on to the big toys of real estate and travel, consider one more feature of the high life that money can buy: an inner circle of cringing ass-kissing sycophants. It is a fact that if you are very rich, powerful, or famous, you will attract people who want to perhaps get some of the money, get favors from your position of power, or take Instagram photos with their famous friend. It means that sooner or later you will be surrounded by people who tell you how great and smart you are all day. Think about that experience. Sooner or later, you will completely lose touch with reality and think that every dumb idea you have is brilliant and no one is as good as you. Every very rich or powerful person experiences this tendency, and some individuals may even have the fiber to resist it. But life is long.

The effect is very real. Chrystia Freeland recounts in her terrible book *Plutocrats* the experience of a US tech executive vacationing at a luxury Four Seasons hotel: "The service was exceptional—at one point, as he was sitting by the pool and dropped the spoon he was using to eat his melon, a waiter instantly appeared with a choice of three differently sized replacement spoons. The Silicon Valley executive said that readjusting to ordinary life had been hard; he had become impatient and rude when confronted by the slightest delay or discomfort. 'When you are used to being catered to twenty-four/seven, you start to feel the world should be built around you and your needs. You lose all sense of perspective.'"[34]

You can tell rich and powerful people have adapted to this bubble of pampering and ball-fondling because anytime someone confronts them to their face, they are stunned. Years have probably gone by since one of their groveling staff dared to jeopardize their job and inner-circle position by contradicting them. When Senator Elizabeth Warren publicly told off megabillionaire media monopolist Michael Bloomberg during the 2020 Democratic primary debates, it was like he had witnessed time travel, he was so dumbstruck. People who are critical of elites—whether celebrities, billionaires, or politicians—tend to get tossed, and soon a powerful groupthinking inner circle is in place.

This tendency is known for leading to many terrible state decisions made by remote leaders who come to believe the pleasing claims of their courtiers, from Bush's invasion of Iraq to Putin's invasion of Ukraine. But I think it also explains how rich people can be reassured when they make really gross decisions, like Elon Musk's blundering purchase and then mangling of Twitter, or indeed his divorcing the mother of his children, who was about his age, and then dating an actress fourteen years younger than he, then another actress fifteen years younger, then a singer seventeen years younger.[35] Obviously the billionaire is aging while his short-lived girlfriends stay the same age—something your friends will give you a lot of shit for, but not if they count on one of your monopolies for a job. Indeed, when the billionaire's texts were revealed during the lawsuit compelling him to buy Twitter, they were pretty cringy: "You are totally right. I 100% agree with you." "I'm ride or die brother—I'd jump on a grande [sic] for you." "I am 100% with you Elon. To the f—cking mattresses no matter what." "You are the hero Gotham needs."[36] The reality of climbing the economic ladder—competitive ass-kissing.

No wonder therapists to the very rich often describe their clients' issues with trust. One psychologist with numerous upper-class clients told the *Guardian*, "I hear this from my clients all the time: 'What do they want from me?'; or 'How are they going to manipulate me?'; or 'They are probably only friends with me because of my money.'"[37] Paranoia is also common—some rich people pay for bulletproof bathroom shower doors.[38]

So really, the ruling class should have its wealth socialized just to help their inner emotional well-being. Socialism is self-care.

Crashing *Mansion*

One of the main arenas for conspicuous consumption is the household. From great stone castles to royal palaces to modern tech-mansions, the rich have long been eager to show just how superior they are to the typical loser living in a shack, tenement, or homeless encampment. And when you're as rich as the owning class, and you have shallow friends to impress, the sky's the limit.

The top end of the US residential property market is completely insane, with over-the-top cutting-edge penthouses and enormous, elaborate Gilded Age mansions. You can keep up with developments in this market segment with the numerous luxury real estate listing services, including the *Wall Street Journal*'s Friday section, *Mansion*. Driven by a combination of elite pride, gloating, and aspirational ogling, these media are how one can learn about Hamptons homes with $30,000 spent on a single room—on the curtains.[39]

Among properties large enough to have names, Casa Encantada is a classic estate in the Bel Air hills outside Los Angeles. The property has the distinction of setting the record for the highest-priced residential property sale in the country—twice, in

1980 and again in 2000. Owned over time by great capitalists like hedge fund boss Ken Griffin and hotel titan Conrad Hilton, the most recent renovation required 250 workers of various specializations. Beyond the gate and long driveway to the motor court with fountain, the breathless real estate coverage describes the "40 rooms, including three kitchens, or 60 if you included the servants' quarters, and the walk-in silver, fur and wine vaults in the basement . . . There were rooms paneled in rare woods like English sycamore and black walnut and furnished with eighteenth century French paintings, antique clocks and centuries-old Chinese porcelains . . . A silver tea service had been made for the czar of Russia in the 1800s."[40] The property was large enough for guests to be "physically tired" after the full tour.

Or consider the once bohemian surfer hideaway of Malibu. For years seen as a less-developed haven with less-crowded beaches than Santa Monica, the area was "discovered" by software billionaire Larry Ellison in the early 2000s, when he began collecting what would become "around 10 homes" in the neighborhood. Celebrities and billionaires followed suit, driving beachfront home prices into the stratosphere. Venture capitalist Marc Andreessen bought three Malibu houses for a quarter billion dollars. Ellison used his enormous fortune to also buy up unassuming rustic local businesses and turn them into chichi sushi restaurants and private clubs, attracting Kardashians but driving out the sunburned California locals. Now, residents complain that most fellow homeowners have two, three, or four other homes and thus visit only occasionally. Even as prices have skyrocketed, the town's full-time population has fallen by a large percentage and school enrollments are less than half their level of twenty years ago.[41]

Ellison, of course, is no stranger to evil land grabs—he bought a Hawaiian island in 2013. On the island of Lanai, Ellison "owns nearly everything on the island, including many of the candy-colored plantation-style homes and apartments, one of the two grocery stores, the two Four Seasons hotels and golf courses, the community center and pool, water company, movie theater, half the roads and some 88,000 acres of land," leaving the "local population . . . one whose economic future is heavily dependent on his decisions."[42]

The Gateses bought a $43 million seaside estate shortly before their divorce, with a "10-person Jacuzzi overlooking a fire pit, a long oceanfront deck, limestone flooring, and a swimming pool."[43] But the pinnacle of today's real estate market, where properties are mostly high-end and become glorified places for the rich to park their incredible wealth, is the laughably gigantic property in the Holmby Hills named "The One" and originally asking half a billion dollars. With twenty bedrooms (including seven for staff in a separate structure), five elevators, and four pools (plus the infinity-edge moat), the huge hyped monstrosity ended up not finding a buyer even at a highly reduced price and sold at bankruptcy auction for a mere $126 million.[44] Other properties by the developer have fared better, including a similarly huge Bel Air mansion that according to the press "comes with two years of prepaid household staff."[45]

Meanwhile, New York City retains the highest concentration of billionaires in the world, as the home of Wall Street and so much of the world's media economy. There, Griffin bought an under-construction penthouse for $238 million, setting a US residential purchase record. Built "after the landlord evicted dozens of middle class tenants from their rent-stabilized apartments," the buyer is not expected to visit frequently. Griffin seems eager to soothe his conscience with large donations that have led to the Whitney art museum naming its new building's lobby after him. The notorious archconservative economics department of the University of Chicago literally renamed the department after Griffin following a $125 million donation.[46] Griffin earned $1.4 billion that year, and has said the rich have "insufficient influence" in politics.

The Gateses' daughter Jennifer paid $51 million for a Tribeca penthouse spanning three floors with the usual two dishwashers, wine fridge, and separate private elevator. The building is marketed as "paparazzi-proof" due to its punched windows and secure underground garage.[47]

Other modern NYC units come with a parking space, since Manhattan is notorious for crowded streets. The cost: one million dollars. "When someone is paying $50 million for an apartment, another $500,000 for the luxury of not walking a block or two and having your own spot, I guess it becomes a rounding error," says the developer.[48] Another favorite of mine is the rich 1950s Manhattanite who directed her butler to return to her Hamptons estate weekly to dig up soil, for her Pekingese, Peaches, to poop on.[49]

But the main destination for today's rich with cash to stash is Billionaires' Row, just south of Manhattan's Central Park. Named after the historic Millionaires' Row of stately properties on the east side of the park, mostly built by the Gilded Age tycoons and since redeveloped, the new developments tend to be unappealing, super-thin, insanely tall residential towers spiking from the city skyline like cell signal bars. Built with unhinged levels of media hype, these towering, charmless buildings are "gilded, gated communities in the sky . . . built with a single constituency in mind: the richest people on earth."[50]

Like many of the properties discussed here, these structures are technically homes "but they are also investment vehicles for the superrich. Some of the owners have never set foot in their apartments, viewing them instead as one might a stock or an artwork from a great master—a vessel in which to store wealth." This tactic is extremely common in the modern housing market, and indeed is widely recognized to play a major role in the grinding housing crisis in major American cities, where surprising numbers of properties sit vacant as third homes, investment properties, or pure poker chips in hedge fund property speculation—all unavailable for any working person to actually dwell within.

Buildings are "jammed with high-end amenities geared to the super rich," like fifteen-thousand-square-foot outdoor terraces, sixty-foot outdoor pools, saunas and steam rooms and basketball courts. But as another worker is quoted in *Doormen*, "Most of them are not like us, they live here sometimes, but they also have houses in London and Hawaii, places like that, you know."[51] One resident of a top-end New York building adds, "Everybody hates each other here."[52]

Many liberal jurisdictions, like New York and London, have recently required developers to include among their mega-ritzy luxury developments some affordable units for normal people, to help cope with the housing shortages racking urban markets. Developers obliged and grudgingly built some middle-class-type units, but still wanted most of their buildings to be the most profitable, high-end model possible, leading them to install special separate entrances for tenants of the more affordable units that became known as "poor doors." The *Guardian* describes a main entrance with "luxury marble tiling and plush sofas, and a sign on the door alert[ing] residents to the fact that the concierge is available. Round the back, the entrance to the affordable homes is a cream corridor, decorated only with grey mail boxes and a poster warning tenants that they are on CCTV and will be prosecuted if they cause any damage."[53] An agent flatly says the separate doors are "so the two social strata don't have to meet."[54]

Other rich people have more classic tastes, preferring stately turn-of-the-century New York City limestone buildings to weird hypermodern towers, and thus find themselves buying town houses and merging them—only to recreate the large Gilded Age mansions the buildings originally were, during the first era of America's ruling class. The *Times* describes these "trophy town-houses": "After spending decades doing duty as schools, embassies, consulates, nonprofit headquarters, apartment houses and the like . . . important and irreplaceable buildings" are now being advertised as "ripe for conversion to what they were in the beginning: beauteous, commodious and expensive single-family residences."[55]

But if any place can contend with Manhattan as a headquarters for the rich, it's the Hamptons, the Long Island beachfront communities a few hours' drive from the city. There the idle rich have more country room to create their visions for their homes. Which, let me tell you, are pretty fucking bonkers. Mining billionaire Ira Rennert's Fair Field estate has sixty-three acres, five buildings including a sixty-six-thousand-square-foot Italianate mansion, twenty-nine bedrooms, three pools, a 164-seat movie theater, and its own power plant.[56]

Another choice instance, regarding a banker's daughter in the 1890s, from Gaines's book on the Hamptons:

> Her gardens were so massive and complex to maintain that every summer she imported thirty gardeners from Japan for the chore, bivouacking them in a small tent city built on a remote corner of the property . . . On occasion, to impress houseguests, Adele would change the entire color of a garden overnight, so guests would wake in the morning to discover a garden of pink flowers where an all-white one had been the night before. To achieve this, Adele's frantic Japanese gardeners uprooted the old garden and planted thousands of water-filled glass vials with cut flowers in them. Because Adele was offended by the sight of the gardeners' toiling in her gardens, her edict was that they had to work only at night. This made their chores rather difficult, especially since the perfection of the gardens was such an obsession with Adele that she decreed they must always look in fresh bloom; so every night the gardeners had to deadhead thousands of fading blooms by lantern or moonlight.[57]

Or consider Ron Perelman, the businessman who built a billion-dollar fortune from the humble beginnings of his father's mere $12 million fortune. His property, The Creeks, is the largest in East Hampton and patrolled by armed guards. Because boaters on the adjacent lake can view the property, Perelman demanded to buy all the rental boats, and when rebuffed asked to purchase the store itself. Gaines relates that "since staff turnover is high (mostly because Perelman frequently fires people), each member of the corps of maids, cooks, handymen, cleaning and grounds maintenance crews, and landscapers is asked to sign a confidentiality agreement. It is also said that the household staff is asked to make themselves scarce if they see Mr. Perelman in passing. Each Friday at a roll call for the staff, a set of dicta and rules are handed out to every employee."[58]

The estate had a storied history, but

Perelman wanted the legendary mansion stripped, renovated, and put back together again from cellar to attic, including the installation of new floors, walls, bathrooms, plumbing, electrical wiring, and ducts for central air-conditioning—in about six weeks. Perelman insisted that he be in residence on weekends to keep an eye on construction, and during the week all the furniture in the house was carried outdoors, covered with tarps, and then carried back inside for him on the weekends. At one point nearly forty painters worked in tandem on the house, the exterior of which changed color several times over the summer until Perelman settled on light beige.[59]

Then there's Mark Zuckerberg's buying spree, occurring around the time his Facebook social media platform was becoming associated with online extremism, election interference, and failure to protect user privacy.[60] According to coverage in the business press, Zuckerberg "looks to buy up neighboring properties to ensure control of his surroundings and likes his homes to be enclosed by foliage to block views from onlookers . . . After buying his five-bedroom home in the Crescent Park area for about $7 million in 2011, he and Ms. Chan bought up four neighboring houses. They paid more than $43 million for all four homes, far above market rate" before razing them. "Real estate agents involved in Mr. Zuckerberg's search were required to sign confidentiality agreements carrying clauses that prohibited them from revealing Mr. Zuckerberg's identity or requiring them to scrub images of properties from the internet." Considering Zuck's poor record of protecting privacy for his billions of users, the *Wall Street Journal* calls his zealous pursuit of privacy for himself "a tad ironic."[61]

More secluded settings are indeed harder for us proles to learn about, but drama sometimes forces open a crack. When Mexico's state oil company chief was wanted for fraud in 2020, he hid out in the southern Spanish enclave of La Zagaleta. Considered "one of the world's most exclusive residential compounds," the estate encompasses two thousand richly landscaped acres with two golf courses. "La Zagaleta is patrolled round the clock by guards and has fences with infrared sensors," and staff "are strictly forbidden to talk about its 230 homeowners or their guests."[62] The oil chief was only arrested when he drove off the estate.

Of course, the rich need help running these gigantic homes. Robert Frank's book *Richistan* describes "butler boot camp" where trainees learn the "Ballet of Service," a smooth dance-like choreography to "become master at the care and feeding of the rich:"

> "They learn how long it takes to clean a 45,000-square-foot mansion (20 to 30 hours depending on the art and antiques) . . . The rich, they will learn, like their shampoo bottles and toothpaste tubes always filled to the top. If their employers have four homes, chances are they'll want their dresser drawers and bathroom cabinets arranged exactly the same in every house, so they don't have to go searching for their socks or pills. And they learn that the rich live in constant fear of germs . . . Most of all, the Starkey students learn never to judge their employers, whom they call 'principals.' If a principal wants to feed her shih tzu braised beef tenderloin steaks every night, the butler should serve it up with a smile. If a principal is in Palm Beach and wants to

send his jet to New York to pick up a Chateau LaTour from his South Hampton cellar, the butler makes it happen, no questions asked."[63]

Senior household staff are today called "household managers," running "family offices" to manage the details of millions in annual spending. The training company also has a manual for principals to learn how to deal with staff, which it calls an "owner's manual."[64]

And when it comes to building up these elite estates, anything goes. Thus:

"Trophy trees" have become the new status symbol for America's uber-rich, with wealthy landowners paying hundreds of thousands of dollars to have the prized plants shipped into their yards by helicopters, barges and flatbed trucks . . . While most wealthy citizens can buy a Bentley or a Rolex, trees—much like original artworks—are one-of-a-kind objects that allow their owner to distinguish themselves and advance their status. Like artworks, the trees are aesthetically pleasing, but they also have the added bonus of being able to signify the owner's environmental credentials and their passion for sustainability . . . Dozens of landscapers can work on any one job, and it can cost clients up to $250,000 for the entire process . . . When [landscapers] approach the original owners of the tree, many are ecstatic about receiving tens of thousands of dollars for an object they believed was relatively worthless. However, he has found many who are unwilling to part with the plants . . . Workers . . . often use a 300-tonne crane to move rip [sic] out the trees from their original location. Given that some of the trees have been in place for more than a century, their roots run deep and the process of removal is at once extremely delicate and incredibly hefty.[65]

Beautiful, precious organisms that take nature centuries to grow are ripped out of the ground so they can be ornaments at the ruling class's ornament-packed estates. Hopefully their spoiled kids at least get some enjoyment from the Given Trees.

To Be, or Yacht to Be

When it comes to conspicuous consumption, sure you need your insanely costly, uncomfortably slick–looking home. But what about when you need to go out? Not on errands of course, your household staff and family shopper will be taking care of that—and who cares what the help goes out in.

But I mean out like joyriding. The yachts of today have gone far beyond the classic sailboat schooners of New England aristocratic families. Today a superyacht is defined as a private, professionally crewed craft longer than eighty feet, of which there are thousands now on the seas, and their rich owners don't much mind the reaction. The St. Barths Bucket yacht race is held every year, including 2009 when the country was seething at Wall Street and its rich proprietors after the enormous banking crisis the year before. *Fortune* magazine called the event "a testament to tone-deafness [and] megawealth . . . If you have sufficient millions, it may not really matter if your portfolio plummets. Nor may you particularly care if the proles are offended by your profligacy."[66]

A top-end model today costs several hundred million bucks, enough to build a couple hospitals, and is the length of a pro football field. Modern units are designed as settings for luxury service, so a model that size may accommodate up to a dozen guests in VIP staterooms but will also have utilitarian bunk-bed dorms for up to thirty crew members, yielding a high crew-to-guest ratio to keep the giant ship sparkling and the guests pampered within an inch of their lives.[67] The Russian oligarch Farkhad Akhmedov's beast has a pair of helipads, a mini-submarine, and a pool across nine decks, although his main goal is keeping it from his ex-wife.[68]

Shipyards catering to the top of the market have order books for superyachts booked out to 2025.[69] And increasingly, these yards are laying down megayachts, luxury ships over 180 feet long, which can only be serviced in certain specialized ports like Barcelona. The ships are so large that they frequently require their own support fleet. The largest ships especially, or those with a more traditional, sailing-based affectation, often require whole additional craft trailing them as they party their way across the Adriatic or the Caribbean. Jeff Bezos's gigantic new 417-foot superyacht has a "support yacht" with its own helipad and extensive stores and water toys, to keep the main craft looking tolerably modest. That main craft cost the Amazon founder a monumental $500 million and created a minor scandal when it was proposed to disassemble a century-old Dutch bridge to allow it to pass.[70]

The yachting technological frontier remains in motion. In 2019 Daniel Snyder, billionaire owner of the Washington Commanders, spent $100 million on the *Lady S*, with the usual insane features—a giant gym capable of golf, basketball, and volleyball, a helipad, spacious guest suites. But his boat made headlines as the first to have a company-certified IMAX theater aboard. The manufacturer reported it added $3 million to the construction cost and in the end, the workers had to build the theater first, then build the rest of the boat around it.[71]

But just because you're a pampered plutocrat cruising the Caribbean doesn't mean you have no problems. An entire consulting market, no joke, now exists for educating yacht crew about very high-end art preservation—because so many billionaires are buying precious, irreplaceable art and putting it on their pleasure ships. Incidents include a champagne cork flying at a Picasso, and a painting by Jean-Michel Basquiat that was "damaged not by sea spray, but by breakfast cereal." The kids threw their cornflakes at the priceless work, "and the crew had made it worse by wiping them off the painting."[72]

The *Guardian* reports that when a client complained a Rothko composition didn't fit in his yacht's grand salon, the consultant sighed: "We turned the piece by 90 degrees. The artist would probably be turning in his grave, but we took a deep breath and said 'It's your painting, do what you like.'" Another had a Japanese modernist piece that didn't fit in the beach club. "In the end we cut it up to make it fit."

Of course it doesn't end for the superrich with play boats. Private jets have become perhaps the definitive symbol of modern wealth, bringing precious exclusivity to help keep you away from the smelly masses, while also maximizing your valuable time. This market has exploded in recent years, motivated by a desire among the rich to avoid what they call the "mosh pit" of boarding commercial airlines.[73] Models vary for private aircraft, with some pitched to the merely affluent who can share access with a jet card, while the top-end Gulfstreams are wholly owned by multibillionaires. The interiors are what you'd expect, with all-plane Wi-Fi installed at a cost of $650,000, and press reports describing "bespoke flatware from Muriel Grateau in Paris, V'Soske rugs or other luxe features."[74]

This book will have a lot more to say about private jets in chapter 5, on the stunning environmental cost of these toys and the consumption habits of the rich generally. For now we'll limit ourselves to perhaps the ultimate private jet experience: travel agencies are now booking trips around the world wholly traveled in private aircraft. Over twenty-four days, travelers will enjoy private flights around the world with luxury, hotel level amenities developed by high-end resorts like the Four Seasons. The *Journal* describes a couple touring: "In Bora Bora, the couple swam with manta rays. In the Wadi Rum desert, they enjoyed a Champagne cocktail 'in the middle of nowhere.' And in Siem Reap, they attended a private ballet performance, hosted by the prince of Cambodia."[75] Newer versions of the itinerary include more remote destinations like New Zealand and the Maldives, including two helicopter excursions, for the easy price of $130,000.

And for luxury air travel, planes aren't the only option. For busy commuters who want to decamp their Silicon Valley or Wall Street jobs to their vacation homes without the bother, yet another industry has arisen to cater to ultra-high-net-worth families: private helicopter travel. For impatient Wall Street financiers especially, money's no object for a ride on a Sikorsky S-76 out to their summer places in the Hamptons. Short rides to the regional airports cost about two hundred bucks for an eight-minute lift, where luxury SUVs await to carry clients to their terminals. "That Noise? It's the 1%, Helicoptering Over Your Traffic Jam," wrote the *New York Times*, adding the industry was "yet another manifestation of the income inequality that has come to define life in a new Gilded Age." One passenger flying to the Hamptons says, "The exclusivity of it, I like that."[76]

And yet the *real* monstrosity is yet another market serving the rich: space tourism. Subject to an insane amount of hype, the space launches that were once the pride of America's public sector are now the playthings of the literally stratospherically rich. As noted in the introduction, three separate billionaires now have their own space programs, some serving military satellite launch clients, and others for space tourism—taking tiny numbers of people sixty-two miles up, to the Kármán line at the very edge of space, to experience a few minutes of weightlessness. The cost is unbelievable, both in money and in emissions.

The market leader is Axiom Space, which uses Elon Musk's SpaceX rockets to dock with the International Space Station, the publicly built orbital research platform. Tickets for the roughly ten days in orbit cost in the neighborhood of $55 million. As in so many cases of market "innovation" (see chapter 4), the innovating is mostly about finding new ways to exploit public resources. The *New York Times* reports: "NASA has in recent years become more receptive to allowing companies to find new ways to make money on the space station . . . NASA set up a price list for various commercial activities, including charging companies like

Axiom $35,000 a night for each tourist staying at a station for space to sleep and the use of its amenities like air, water, the internet and the toilet. The largest chunk of the $55 million ticket price is for the rocket ride, which Axiom will pay to SpaceX, not NASA."[77] Rich non-astronauts have already visited in the past, as when the Japanese billionaire Yusaku Maezawa went up in a Russian rocket in 2021.[78]

The big trial for Jeff Bezos's own Blue Origin tourism company came in the summer of that year when after an endless media circus, Bezos and a few chosen passengers successfully reached the edge of space and then returned to sea level, over about ten minutes. The affair was seen as risky as space tourism vehicles are subject to far, far less testing than components of commercial flights.[79] The later death of a billionaire and his entourage on the *Titan* submersible shows the drastic potential of ruling-class thrill-seeking, but Bezos was unscathed.[80] Amusingly, one auction winner who'd bid $28 million was a no-show due to a "scheduling conflict," a good term for chickening out on a billionaire's roll of the dice.[81]

Richard Branson, UK billionaire and founder of Virgin Atlantic and spin-off travel businesses, was excited to beat Bezos to the punch that summer by launching his space tourism venture first, charging a quarter-million dollars for the experience.[82] He is said to have celebrated on his private island in the British Virgin Islands, although the regrettable failure of his Virgin Orbit subsidiary, which was to launch satellites from under the wings of a modified Boeing 747, may have dampened his mood.[83] Socialist writer Luke Savage described these operators as "a class of people whose fortunes have grown so incomprehensibly large they must now be spent on yachts that contain other yachts and vanity expeditions in the thermosphere because the traditional symbols of billionaire opulence no longer suffice."[84]

The basic picture is as clear as a classic painting on a superyacht. By now the reader must see the regrettable necessity of throwing the rich overboard.

Art of the Deal for Art

It's well known now that rich households are willing to pay stunning amounts for fine art. A Warhol went for $105 million in 2013, a Francis Bacon triptych for $142 million (it ended up on a yacht), even Norman Rockwell's famous *Saying Grace* sold for $46 million. Art market analysts note that the taste of rich investors in art is often more keyed to its expected performance as an investment, but of course elite buyers also need to be told they have impeccable taste. Some genres of art, like postwar American art, French impressionist works, or paintings by Old Masters, have incredible, competitive demand from rich buyers, while whole realms of great art held in high esteem by scholars receive no bids.[85]

A truly classic episode in today's art market was triggered by a nighttime attic fire at The Creeks, Perelman's infamous overbuilt Hamptons estate. The fire caused significant damage to the structure, and various expensive artworks were evacuated, although in protective "museum quality" cases. The art never burned or got soaked in the water from the fire hoses dousing it, but afterward Perelman sued his insurers, claiming he "noticed some changes." He claimed one "didn't have its spark," adding, "It just lost—it just lost its oomph."[86]

Richer still, Perelman's insurance underwriters, including at the great Lloyd's of London, had to admit in court that "Mr. Perelman had been allowed in his policy to set valuations for artworks he owned, a consideration he had asked to be afforded 'as a collector,'" as the press reported. "A collector with billions of dollars" would be more suggestive of why this crazy policy was extended.

Similarly, casino magnate Steve Wynn was showing off his *Le Rêve* by Picasso to his awful guests and put his elbow through the canvas. Wynn, who has a diagnosed eye condition, then sued Lloyd's, who agreed they were on the hook for the lost value of the painting but couldn't agree on how much they owed.[87] Ultimately the canvas was restored and Wynn sold it to the financier Steven

Cohen for $155 million. Picasso, a socialist himself, would probably be just totally pleased.

But the daily reality of what the rich have done to art is bad enough. The business press reports that a handful of ugly warehouse complexes now have some of the best art collections in the world, because that is where the owning class stores art bought as an investment. The utilitarian Geneva free port zone, a maze of warehouses, railroad tracks, and barbed-wire fences, contains "treasures from the glory days of ancient Rome. Museum-quality paintings by Old Masters. An estimated 1,000 works by Picasso. As the price of art has skyrocketed, perhaps nothing illustrates the art-as-bullion approach to contemporary art collection habits more than the proliferation of warehouses like this one, where masterpieces are increasingly being tucked away by owners more interested in seeing them appreciate than hanging on walls."[88] Originally for storing bulk commodities like grain, free ports are becoming "storage lockers for the superrich," even as actual museums, where the public can view some of the human artistic legacy, are under threat from budget-cutting austerity. The director of the Louvre calls the ports the greatest museums no one can see, and confidentiality rules mean that now little is known about where various beloved compositions even are. The *Times* notes Picasso's *Garçon à la pipe* disappeared after being bought in a Sotheby's auction in 2004 for $104 million. "Dealers suspect a free port is its likely new home."

Stamping Your Classport

But of course, the rich lifestyle is about a lot more than just expensive, extra-fancy versions of consumer goods we all buy some version of. Any person of means will tell you they've learned money is better spent on experiences and travel than goods, and travel itself is an indelible feature of elite life. But it's a lot more than the summer trip to European tourist traps that the average Joe counts himself lucky to get. C. Wright Mills wrote in *The Power Elite,* "All over the world, like lords of creation, are those who, by travel, command the seasons and, by many houses, the very landscape they will see each morning or afternoon they are awakened."[89]

Consider further the practice of buying passports. Today fourteen countries offer passports with a qualifying real estate investment. Spain's property visa program, for example, has a minimum investment of €500,000. Many more countries, including the US and most of the EU, offer residence visas for non-property investors, which can frequently lead to passports over time. A number of smaller states, plus Turkey, will directly issue passports to property buyers regardless of residence. The *Times* notes, "The picky passport shopper needs to consider price, each country's tax system and the speed of its bureaucracy: Dominica is the fastest to hand over a passport, and Turkey the slowest among nations that go straight to a passport . . . Wealthy Chinese are by far the biggest buyers of both visas and passports, followed by Russians, experts say. There is also growing interest among French citizens eager to avoid high income taxes and Britons desperate to maintain their European Union membership."[90] A consultant estimates that 36 percent of UHNWIs (those with assets over $30 million) have a second passport.

There's more, but this book only has so much space. The elite consumption habits of the very rich are an object of fascination in media, so you can always catch a cable TV show or YouTube channel that tours giant coastal mansions or outlines the luxe features on new superyachts. With a mix of stunned resentment and deluded envy, there will always be an audience for the lifestyles of the rich and famous.

But let's remember the monumental opportunity cost of this consumption. Every one of those million-dollar watches and $100 million estates could have been spent on housing and health care for normal human use. The US government has estimated that housing all America's homeless would cost roughly $20 billion, or forty Bezos-yachts.[91] Pouring resources into rich-kid toys is the opposite of what a rational economic system would be doing at this time of troubles for the world.

The rich have exploited us and the world's resources for a tremendous fortune that has been largely squandered on flashy shit for shallow show-offs. That money should be used by the rest of us. Who the "rest of us" are is the subject of the next chapter.

CHAPTER 3
THE CLASSES

HIERARCHIES OF CAPITALISM

Of course, I have as much power as the president has.
—**Bill Gates**[1]

To serve is to rule.
—**Motto, Groton School**[2]

Having delved deep into the incredible hoarding of wealth at the top, and the bottomless ocean of money-wasting conspicuous consumption, the average Joe on the street might ask, "Where the hell do I fit into this?"

Well, a ruling class needs classes to rule over, and that's what we turn to now. Lower classes have a history as long as civilization and are an enduring feature of hierarchical, class-based societies. Roman plebians, Greek slaves, China's untold generations of poor farm families, the grubby working class of Victorian England—there are endless configurations for the lower rungs of society. But capitalism, like any system, has unique characteristics of life for the less-fabulously-wealthy majority.

Of course, there are many valid ways to dissect and study a society, by region or by race or by age or by gender. But the way economic resources are distributed through a country, and how that puts different people in social positions of power or submission, has a lot to tell you about what happens in that society. Class is a lot more than a tax bracket; it is kind of social world created simply by a few people being in a position to grant or retract the ability of the great working class to make a living, and the twisted relationships that creates among people.

This is a book on the ruling class, but here we'll focus on the object of its power, which remains anyone who works for a living—the global working class.

Time to declassify the class structure.

Bottom Dollars

Broadly, an observer of the economy can make out a number of social and economic levels, not only based on how much money people have but how they make their living. This book has so far covered the economics of the richest households, whose members may work, and often earn gigantic CEO incomes from managing large corporate entities. But primarily the household incomes of these families are made up of income from *property*—dividends on stocks, rent on residential or commercial properties, interest income from big cash deposits, and capital gains from corporate stock buybacks.

This is the crucial distinction between the rich, or the owning class, and the rest of us. Most of us make our money from working, but for the rich this is only sometimes the case. The ability to not just have a giant income, but to have a giant income from assets your family already owns, is an economically existential distinction. It's crucial to recall the numbers on stock ownership, where the richest 1 percent of households owns 40 percent of traded corporate stock, and the top 10 percent owns 84 percent.[3] This position of ownership of the productive economy, and the social and political power arising from that, is what defines the ruling class, and it goes back centuries to the advent of capitalism in the enclosure movement. Economist Douglas Dowd recalls the origin of capitalism in "the exploitation of workers whose farming land had been commodified by 'the enclosure movement.' Those who had worked the land, free but far from rich, were swept off the land . . . and were transformed into desperate and powerless laborers."[4] The land became private property, its new owners the ruling class.

Below the elite are various economic echelons that people often enjoy smooshing together into a vague "middle class." Historically, analysts on the Left have called the rest of society the "working class," which has the advantage of suggesting something important—most families pay the bills by working, earning wages per hour or salaries per year in exchange for labor. The kind of labor varies greatly, but from elite software coders to sewer maintenance workers, work is being done for an employer in order to make a living.

However, many people—especially those who don't want anyone to focus on the monumental wealth and power of the rich—prefer to blur this simple distinction. While conservative supporters of capitalism and "free enterprise" enjoy claiming they oppose vague "elites," these elites usually turn out to be various nonconservative middle-class people, like college professors and media figures. An actual billionaire may be thrown in *if* they aren't conservative, like George Soros or Tom Steyer.

These voices also like to suggest the main class difference is between blue- and white-collar work, roughly manual labor and intellectual work. And indeed, there is a dramatic difference in the daily work lives of a worker manipulating a spreadsheet in a climate-controlled office and a blue-collar worker toiling to clean a hideous "fatberg" of congealed material in a sewer under our feet, or climbing overhead to mind-bending heights on cell phone towers taller than skyscrapers with little protection.

But for all their major differences, blue-collar and white-collar workers all have one pivotal thing in common: the threat of a pink slip. Anyone working for one of the enormous companies that dominate most economic sectors can be laid off in the event of a recession or other retrenching, no matter how important your work is or how well you're paid for it. The exact details of how to define classes remains a fluid debate.[5] But fundamentally, anyone in the white-collar or blue-collar working class, however exactly you define them, is at the mercy of the boss and the company's quarterly profit-per-share targets. This is why class is a useful concept—as researcher Katie Quan has said, "Not to think in terms of class is unfortunate, since no matter what our ideological persuasion may be, class analysis gives us a way of viewing the world that identifies power relationships. It clarifies who has power."[6]

Class shouldn't be so controversial—capitalists talk about it all the time. When told one of his schemes to crush competitors was illegal, early railroad monopolist Cornelius Vanderbilt memorably said, "What do I care about the law? Hain't I got the power?"[7] A century later, PC operating system monopolist Bill Gates said, "Of course, I have as much power as the president has."[8]

The Marxist economist Douglas Dowd addresses the question of what power is: "The short answer is that social power is held by those who control what is . . . most valued in their society . . . Control over the means of material survival has placed its possessors at the center of power in all societies. In the modern world the key has been private ownership and control over the means of production; the very definition of capitalism."[9] C. Wright Mills wrote in his famous book *The Power Elite* that "Class consciousness is not equally characteristic of all levels of American society: it is most apparent in the upper class . . . Those of the upper strata . . . if only because they are fewer in number, are able with much more ease to know more about one another . . . and thus to be conscious of their own kind. They have the money and the time required to uphold their common standards."[10]

And while liberal social analysis often relies on a pluralist approach, seeing companies and workers as just a few among many social groups deserving an equal political hearing, in fact the interests of the workforce and the business community are almost entirely irreconcilable—a raise for the workers means a cut in company profit. Sociologist Erik Olin Wright observed in *Understanding Class* that "the economic advantages people get from being in a privileged class position are *causally connected* to the disadvantages of people excluded from those class positions . . . [T]he rich are rich in part *because* the poor are poor; the rich do things to secure their wealth that contribute to the disadvantages poor people face in the world."[11]

All this suggests that regardless of the real divergences of blue- or white-collar jobs, anyone below the owning class is truly working class. But it also recognizes the owning class is in a position of major power over us, who work for our damn living, and there are pretty big ramifications of the concentrated ownership of wealth amassed by those at the top of the social order. If the world's productive farmland, car factories, oil refineries, data storage centers, and pharmaceutical patents are owned by a small minority of rich people, it puts the rest of us into a position of almost inevitable dependence. The huge majority of us don't have the land to grow our own food or the ability to produce our own essential products. All we can do is work for the firms holding these productive assets, essentially renting ourselves to them in exchange for a paycheck. But not only are we subject to firing at any moment, we're also unlikely to get the full value of our labor since everyone else is in the same position.

This situation means competition among workers for jobs, which suppresses pay and benefits for everyone—demand too much, and some other poor shmuck with kids to feed may underbid you. Private ownership also means that a company (or its rich owners) can up and move their factories or other capital holdings across the country or around the world. The owners therefore have incredible power in their hands, power that allows them to demand workers must submit to the worldwide workplace hierarchy where the ruling class of shareholders hires a CEO to tell managers to tell workers what to do.

Many supporters of capitalism don't see this as a problem, since multiple employers exist and anyone can always start their own business. However, thanks to neoliberal deregulation in the 1980s and '90s, many industries are more and more monopolized, limiting employment options. Further, starting your own business of any size means competing against these giants, and often requires a bank loan, banks being businesses with stockowners just like other companies. These facts put workers, whether educated professionals or toiling laborers, in a vulnerable position relative to the rich owners of productive property (what economists call capital).

So while conservative thinkers behold the labor market and see freedom and liberty, in fact we are in a position of stealth domination by the rich who own so much of our world's resources. I wrote a whole book taking up the question of capitalism and freedom in detail, but suffice it to say that the realistic life options for the average jerk on the street is utterly dwarfed by the wide range of action available to the gigantic corporations and rich family fortunes that tower over us.[12] It's difficult to seriously claim that people are free when they're subject to sudden decisions that can put them out of a job, or into a worse or more dangerous one, based on a rich man's whim. And in markets, "there is something wrong when people have vastly different numbers of dollar ballots to cast in market elections," as the great socialist economist Robin Hahnel wrote, leading medicine to provide more cosmetic surgery for shallow rich people and less basic medical care for poor families, who lack the dollar votes to make it economical.[13]

Unprofessional

The blue- and white-collar split does matter, even if the fundamental distinction is between those whose income comes from work and those whose income comes from property. For example, the blue-collar working class has been devastated by the outsourcing of industrial manufacturing from the US and other developed countries. In the developed world, employers may have to pay for outrageous luxuries like health insurance, and in the 1980s and '90s moved production to developing countries with far lower pay expectations. Free trade deals greatly eased the process for global companies to "offshore" or "internationally outsource" production, and the trend became enormous—a study by Harvard Business School found *84 percent* of a very large sample of US firms moved production offshore in 2011.[14]

The loss of millions of good-paying manufacturing jobs has just utterly destroyed working-class communities around the world, including in the US. These are the parts of the country being decimated by fentanyl and other opiates, the ones without any realistic economic opportunities to keep people off the street. In 1995, when the process was in full swing, the corporate magazine *Businessweek* noted that "of course, companies always try to restrain labor costs to maximize profits. But when unemployment falls, they're usually forced to raise wages to attract and retain employees. That's not happening this time," because companies "have access to . . . pools of cheaper labor in other parts of the globe."[15] Over time, professional-class jobs like accountancy and engineering have become vulnerable to the process as well.

But the visible distinction between white- and blue-collar work has created opportunities to blur the much more profound distinction between the ruling class and working class, and allows supporters of the status quo to give great prominence to intra-working-class divisions. For example, during the first year of COVID the *Wall Street Journal* called the blue-collar/white-collar split a "Deep Divide Between Haves and Have-Nots."[16] When the COVID-19 epidemic hit, many office workers could work from home, submitting work online and meeting through videoconferencing software. Working-class people, from cashiers to meat plant workers to bus drivers to utility workers, stayed on the job and often paid with their health or their lives.

Some observers have developed different terms for the blue- and white-collar strata within the working-class population. The term "professional-managerial class" is sometimes used to refer to better-paid workers who often hold a college degree or other credential proving the possession of skilled knowledge. The expression indicates their positions as professionals—doctors, lawyers, engineers, professors, scientists—or working in management, that echelon of business employees who work for the business owner but give orders to the rest of the workforce. This PMC is then contrasted with the more common use of working class: those doing more physical work or considered to be less skilled (or anyway not requiring a formal degree, although often an extreme amount of work knowledge and training is involved).

The sadly late socialist writer and cocreator of the PMC concept, Barbara Ehrenreich, had this to say about the professional-managerial class in her book *Fear of Falling*: Professionals often believe their education and skills put them on track to climb a ladder into the rich class, but

> the professional middle class is still only a *middle* class, located well below the ultimate elite of wealth and power. Its only "capital" is knowledge and skill, or at least the credentials imputing such skill and knowledge. And unlike real capital, these cannot be hoarded against hard times, preserved beyond the lifetime of an individual, or, of course, bequeathed... Whether the middle class looks down toward the realm of less, or up toward the realm of more, there is the fear, always, of falling.[17]

As recognition has spread among the public of the astronomical riches and overwhelming influence of the ruling class, there has been a growing admission among prominent media that perhaps there *is* class conflict after all, but it is only among these two strata, the manually laboring working class and the college-educated professional class. And there are, as we've already seen, real differences beyond work conditions, as anyone who has worked in both levels can tell you. But the people claiming a great clash between educated and non-college-educated middle-class families are usually conservatives and liberals who support private property and capitalism, and who usually discourage class-based thinking. They seem to have discovered their inner Marxists now that the rich are nearly universally seen as too loaded and powerful, and would probably like to redirect our significant class resentments. Divide and conquer has been a formidable tool historically and today.

This strategy also draws on people's desire, in our current economic system, to feel like they have people to look down on, to prove they are not the losers of society. The "middle class" term encourages people to think they're not in the bottom rungs, which speaks to an anxiety common in hierarchy-based societies like ours. "Hey, I'm middle class, maybe not yet rich but I'm not one of those loser poors." There's a strong social need for that among many people, especially when every institution we have is organized around who's giving orders and who follows them.

Further, this book has already mentioned the decline in US life expectancy, a stunning development for a country so lousy with wealth. But it's well recognized in epidemiological circles that this decline is mainly among the white working class, confirmed by research in one of the most respected scientific journals in the country, the *Proceedings of the National Academy of Sciences*. In 2021 it published research confirming "life expectancy in adulthood is falling for those without a BA degree," finding the one-third of Americans with a bachelor's degree live not just more prosperous but longer lives, and this was true regardless of gender or race. Incredibly, "by 2018, intraracial college divides were larger than interracial divides conditional on college; by our measure, those with a college diploma are more alike one another irrespective of race than they are like those of the same race who do not have a BA."[18]

Professionals with college degrees are also well known to have better incomes, which makes a major difference in quality of life. Professional jobs are typically less physically demanding than blue-collar work, although PMC workers often have the heavily encouraged idea that their comfortable but relatively modest incomes are just the beginning of their upward climb. However, class mobility, as this idea is known, has been declining in the US for years— the conservative *Wall Street Journal* reports on a "substantial body of research" finding "at least 45% of parents' advantage in income is passed along to their children, and perhaps as much as 60%."[19] Children in poorer families are commonly in poor health, which is well established to have lifelong effects on both adult health and economic outcomes—slum housing, for example, is far more likely to contain lead paint and water pipes, which do long-lasting damage to juvenile nervous systems and brain development. Asthma is far more common among poorer households whose kids inhale mold, dust mites, and other harmful domestic toxins in poorly maintained or cleaned housing.[20] Ironically, class mobility is now lower in the US than in the countries of Scandinavia, which, despite often being insulted for being too socialist, invest heavily in public goods like quality education and health care, which improve mobility.

Despite it all, class mobility retains a mystique, especially in the US, and college plays arguably the central role in that mythology. Colleges today are encouraged to have first-generation college students among their graduating classes, and education can enable a working-class kid to become a professional-class adult, if they wish. The admissions process is fraught for professional families, with great pressure to get their child into the right school, and beyond the specific category of racial preferences through affirmative action (now ended anyway by the Supreme Court), admissions and college success have been broadly seen to be a meritocracy, similar to the market itself.

Which is why the Varsity Blues scandal was such a psychological blow to the professional class. A college consultant ran a business getting kids of wealthy families into prestigious schools on fraudulent grounds. Methods included cheating on tests using special accommodations, fake athletic backgrounds to get sports scholarships, and sometimes bribing coaches. The consultant was recorded on an FBI wiretap saying to a complicit parent living on the coast, "I'll make them a sailor or something, because of where you live."[21] Because some of the parent clients were famous celebrities and the truly wealthy, the scandal caught especially big headlines. The $25 million fraudulent business led to a modest prison sentence.

But the case also exposed how colleges themselves badger wealthy families for fundraising, blurring the line between legal collegiate donations and bribes. The significance of this came out in a new research report on college admissions using an enormous dataset from the most prestigious schools, including the Ivy League, Stanford, Duke, MIT, and the University of Chicago, covering half a million applicants. It found, as the New York Times summarized, even among students with the same test scores, "children from families in the top 1 percent were 34 percent more likely to be admitted than the average applicants, and those from the top 0.1 percent were more than twice as likely to get in ... [C]olleges gave preference to the children of alumni and to recruited athletes, and gave children from private schools higher nonacademic ratings."[22] The result shows "how America's elite colleges perpetuate the intergenerational transfer of wealth and opportunity ... [T]hese policies amounted to affirmative action for the children of the 1 percent, whose parents earn more than $611,000 a year." Public universities were found to be much more fair, but elite colleges play a disproportionate role in government and corporate decision-making—while less than 1 percent of US college students attend the top twelve schools, 13 percent of the top 0.1 percent of earners attended them, along with 12 percent of Fortune 500 senior executives and a quarter of the US Senate.

After college, your life as a consumer may also be dramatically easier if you come from a more affluent middle-class background. The business press has reported for years on CLV—consumer lifetime value. This is a class of measurements used in the business world that employs various economic and behavioral cues to sort consumers into different categories. Companies in turn base their offers of service and pricing on these categories. If you have a smartphone or bank account, you have at least a couple of these ratings, and like the various competing corporate credit scores each one of us is so lucky to have, these things shape your consumer options, like credit card perks or upgrade options for airline seats. If you call to complain frequently, if you make a lot of returns, if you wait for things to go on sale before buying, you may be considered a "costly consumer" with too low of a lifetime value to the company to be worth catering to—your calls will go to the lowest-rated centers and have the longest wait times. Some of the systems assume married people are better customers, some assume the opposite, and of course your score is secret and not available to you. The business press quotes a Wharton School marketing professor who comments, "Not all customers deserve a company's best efforts."[23]

This is the real economics of class levels. Other works on the subject are playful treatments of mostly personal class signals, like Paul Fussell's enduringly popular book, *Class*. Still surprisingly current on campuses, it describes how to tell a middle-class person from a working-class person, mostly using clothing and media cues. It has a funny appendix including exercises challenging you to rank people or households by visible class signals, mainly relying on broad class stereotyping and a monumental snobbishness.[24] While very entertaining and a popular favorite, it is the only book on the subject of class I have ever read with no economics in it, although it is rich on the cosmetics of class hierarchies.

Blue- and white-collar details aside, the basic reality of concentrated property, property needed by living humans in order to produce the needs of life, creates the fundamental class dynamic of today. Workers getting a pay raise often comes with a fall in the value of their employer's stock, since the company will be less profitable going forward because a few more pennies will be going to the working class. This means, in short, that there is a relation of enduring class conflict in capitalism, between the rich who own the economic means of production, and various tiers of working people who have the choice of working for them, or watching the kids starve. Now that's a class line.

Don't take my word for it! It was the great Warren Buffett, multibillionaire and one of the world's richest men, who frankly admitted, "There is class warfare, all right, but it's my class, the rich class, that's making war, and we're winning."[25]

Buyer's Remorse

So far this discussion of the classes has focused on the distribution of wealth and its consequences for everyone else. But this owning class needs to be connected to the one institution that's a match for global corporate power—the state.

It's an easy connection to draw. Historically, the governing elites of many civilizations have been synonymous with wealth— John Kampfner notes in his sweeping book on the rich throughout history that the word "rich" shares an Indo-European root word with the Latin term *rex* and the Sanskrit *rajah*, both meaning "king."[26] Early monarchs used their control of the state to monopolize economic resources (mainly land- and slave-based in that era), and systems like feudalism were based on parceling out local control over portions of their lands to nobles or aristocrats who in turn ruled over the luckless peasants. Thorstein Veblen observed that this means the rich are naturally conservative, since they benefit the most from current arrangements and have the most to lose if they are changed in some way.[27]

The United States, since its origins the most thoroughly capitalist country in the world, shows how much power free markets can create for the rich owners of big firms, but also how completely controlled by money and commerce a government can be. The country's first chief justice of the Supreme Court, John Jay, wrote: "Those who own the country ought to run it."[28]

With the advent of industrial capitalism in the 1800s, incredible economic power independent of the state emerged, to such an extent that by the late nineteenth century, figures like John Rockefeller and Cornelius Vanderbilt could fully control corrupt state legislatures, buy judges' rulings with favors, and largely write legislation as needed—although the main goal, especially in countries like the US that have little precapitalist history, was to keep the state from meddling in markets, or worse, blocking the consolidation of markets into gigantic private empires like Rockefeller's Standard Oil. Once the markets are monopolized, sure, some state regulation is pleasing to the rich, as its costs are easily met by the incumbent titanic firms but are burdensome to upstart competitors. Matthew Josephson's *The Robber Barons* recounts how early railroads protected their regional monopolies—their owners "went to the state or national capital with a valise of greenbacks; or . . . sat directly in Congress . . . giving out stock to other Congressmen that they might be prompted to look after their own property. [California rail baron] Collis Huntington, to be sure, was a subtle master, who whenever possible secured signed evidence, such as canceled checks given in payment, so that the men involved were 'ever afterward my slaves.'"[29]

Sociologist Stanley Aronowitz wrote that "the term *ruling* class signifies the power bloc that at any given historical period exercises economic and political dominance . . . over the society as a whole and over the class within which it functions . . . [T]he dominant fraction of capital tends to play the leading role together with the top layer of the permanent political class."[30] Likewise the socialist journalist Doug Henwood defines the ruling class in *Jacobin* magazine as that "politically engaged capitalist class, operating through lobbying groups, financial support for politicians, think tanks, and publicity, that meshes with a senior political class that directs the machinery of the state . . . [W]e shouldn't underestimate the importance of the political branch of the ruling class in shaping the thinking of the capitalists, who are too busy making money to think much on their own or even organize in their collective interest."[31] Henwood's point speaks to how fundamental a firm control over the government is to any ruling class.

In the industrial revolution of the latter 1800s, the original monopolists like Rockefeller and J. P. Morgan, along with their political counterparts from President McKinley to Ronald Reagan, were mostly WASPs—a term used to refer to the ruling class being dominated by white Anglo-Saxon Protestants. Henwood argues in *Harper's* that for all their crimes here and around the world, the WASPs had at least the virtue of taking a long-term view of their possessions; today's ruling class, while more diverse, has no such overarching project besides enrichment. This reminds of C. Wright Mills's point that "no matter what its pretensions, the American upper class is merely an enriched bourgeoisie . . . [T]hey cannot invent an aristocratic past where one did not exist."[32] The WASPs did try though—Henwood notes the famous slogan of Groton, the hyper-elite Massachusetts boarding school that taught corporate and political elites from FDR to the Bush dynasty, is *Cui servire est regnare*: "To serve is to rule."[33]

However, this overlap of state and capital often leads misguided supporters of capitalism, like today's libertarians, to chalk up any monopolies in the economy to "crony capitalism"—government figures instituting laws or regulations that put an industry under the control of one person or company that is politically allied with them. This is indeed a quite common phenomenon in the world today, especially in the developing world, as chapter 6 will explore. But there were no regulations giving Rockefeller the insane power of an oil monopoly, no senator gifted Carnegie his near-monopoly in steel, and no regulation granted Google its mobile search monopoly. Natural market forces operating in gloriously unregulated businesses led to these monopolies and oligopolies, through well-known market dynamics like economies of scale, network effects, and the lasting appeal of market power.[34]

Much has been written on the fascinating reasons capitalist competition leads to market consolidation and monopoly, and the endnotes for this section include great reading on the subject. But for the moment suffice it to say, as the great socialist writer and critic of totalitarianism George Orwell did, that "a return to 'free' competitions means for the great mass of people a tyranny probably worse, because more irresponsible, than that of the State. The trouble with competitions is that somebody wins them. [Prominent conservative economist] Professor Hayek denies that free capitalism necessarily leads to monopoly, but in practice that is where it has led."[35] And within those towering monopolies, the workplace is a strict legal hierarchy. As Ehrenreich wrote, "Some employers bar speech of any kind with your fellow employees . . . You probably had to pee in a cup to get your job . . . [Y]our purse or backpack can be searched by the employer at any time; your e-mails and Web activity can be monitored."[36]

But in my view, the definitive story of the dominance of capital over the state comes from the treasury crisis of 1894, when financial shifts had undermined the US dollar to the point that the US Treasury had to acquire fresh overseas gold reserves to back the currency. The tale is told by Josephson:

> In 1894 the Secretary of the Treasury, with Cleveland's consent, had been compelled to go to Morgan to borrow $50,000,000 for the purchase of foreign gold. Morgan had thundered "Impossible!"—that is, save at his own terms, which he ultimately forced the government in its extremities

to accept . . . By mobilizing a powerful coterie of banks, life insurance and trust companies the Corsair had succeeded in financing the government's needs and "saving his country" at usurious rates . . . But "saving the country" once had been insufficient; the gold had been drained away rapidly again by the great hoarders, the gold reserve had vanished anew. Cleveland, under fire for his dealings with the banking consortium, had been forced nevertheless to come, hat in hand, for a further issue of gold bonds, in 1895, at terms imposed by the Morgan syndicate . . . Fearful of popular opinion, the President had resisted paying the "pound of flesh" exacted. The story has often been told of how Morgan, rebuffed by the President, waited alone and played solitaire at his hotel in Washington, massively silent, stubborn in his certainty—as the government's gold reserve sank to only a day's supply—that Cleveland, having no other refuge, must in the end submit once more to him, the master of Wall Street. . . . At a subsequent Congressional hearing, asked the profits made from the affair, "I decline to answer."[37]

What is political power? I put it to you it is being able to bail out the entire United States government. Twice.

In the modern period, participating in politics takes resources—time, money, and energy. Thomas Ferguson of the University of Massachusetts refers to "the 'Golden Rule' of political analysis—to discover who rules, follow the gold," in this context meaning "trace the origins and financing of the campaign." Ferguson's main point is that "the investment theory of parties holds that parties are more accurately analyzed as *blocs of major investors who coalesce to advance candidates representing their interests.*"[38] No sector of society has more time and money to invest than the business world and great capitalists, but Ferguson suggested labor unions could help regular people participate in the political process by making it easier and more fun to invest time and energy in politics.

On the one hand, government power has the force of law, and states can force capitalists to pay taxes or break up their corporate monopolies. Then again, modern states often have strict legal limits for the power of various state officeholders, from term limits to disclosure rules to the balance of powers with other government arms. The power of money, on the other hand, can grow without any limit and put just incredible power in the hands of its owner. If you're a megalomaniac who wants power, sure you could join the state and have very real but limited power. Or you could become a billionaire and buy your own news networks and newspapers, shaping the ideas people hear, and then move your wealth around the world when a state displeases you (rewarding another one that wouldn't dare tax your ninth vacation home in the process). This ability to yank money away from states with displeasing governments, or "capital flight," is itself a major check on any political success by the Left; at the first sign of social democracy, the ultrarich can sell off a country's bonds and currency to crash its growth prospects.

When the enormous housing bubble exploded in 2008 and touched off the greatest financial crisis since the Great Depression, it became a lasting source of public bitterness when Congress and the Federal Reserve ran gigantic bailout programs for the huge, deregulated banks that had placed bad bets on the market. The megabanks, as they are known, were far too large to be allowed to default (which would have resembled the events of the 1930s), but rather than break them back up or nationalize them the government gave them over $700 billion in bailout money, plus years of cheap loans from the Fed, while the public received little beyond unemployment checks in the resulting deep, long recession.

The bailout was arranged by the banker-run Treasury Department of the George W. Bush administration, but was continued by Barack Obama. When Obama used harsh terms to criticize Wall Street's reckless housing bets at a time of growing public resentment, Wall Street traders who had contributed to his campaign openly used the term "buyer's remorse"—we invested in this guy, and he's saying rude things![39] The fact that he sustained their bail-outs and let Congress, where the industry has great influence, write their own reregulation apparently wasn't enough to make the deal worth it.[40] At this time *Businessweek* ran the headline "Finance Executives Are Confused About Why the Nation Loathes Them."[41] In the end, both political parties remained dependent on Wall Street, whose donor role only grew in the years after the huge crash. Unsurprisingly, little was done to seriously impinge on their power and privilege.[42]

When a new, smaller but still important set of regional lenders imploded due to abrupt depositor flight in 2023, a similar political response occurred. Many of these banks catered to cash-rich venture capitalists in the tech sector, and with them teetering in the midst of bank runs, the FDIC—the government-run deposit insurance program—announced it would waive the historic deposit cap of $250,000. Writer Nathan Robinson observed in a headline for the socialist magazine *Current Affairs* that "Every Libertarian Becomes a Socialist the Moment the Free Market Screws Them."[43]

And in the nuts and bolts of the Republic, money is a dominating force, especially following the Supreme Court's infamous Citizens United ruling in 2010, which allowed unlimited contributions and spending by super PACs in political campaigns. Since then, it has been up to invaluable nonprofits like the Center for Responsive Politics to allow the public to keep track of who has paid money to which politician's campaigns. Using this data, it was revealed in 2021 that "a dozen megadonors and their spouses contributed a combined $3.4 billion to federal candidates and political groups since 2009, accounting for nearly one out of every 13 dollars raised," as the *New York Times* summarized.[44] The biggest single spender was the media monopolist, billionaire, former New York City mayor, and monumental asshole Michael Bloomberg, who spent $1.4 billion. Although a full billion of that was on his own vanity presidential campaign.

Developments like these led the popular socialist senator Bernie Sanders to ask Treasury Secretary Janet Yellen in a congressional hearing, "In your judgement, given the enormous power held by the billionaire class and their political representatives, are we still a capitalist democracy or have we gone over to an oligarchic form of society in which incredible enormous economic and political power now rests with the billionaire class?" Yellen declined to answer directly.[45]

Socialist philosopher Olúfẹ́mi O. Táíwò argues that institutions like the state are subject to "elite capture," where "political projects can be hijacked in principle or in effect by the well positioned and resourced . . . Elite capture happens when the advantaged few steer resources and institutions that could serve the many toward their own narrower interests and aims . . . Elite capture is symptomatic of social systems with unequal balances of power."[46] Whole arms of state policy, from housing to foreign aid, get hugely twisted by this process and often end up further enriching financiers, and demoralizing activists. But there are ways to fight back.

Classes and Clashes

Many people in the lower rungs of the capitalist hierarchy don't especially enjoy suffering in penniless poverty when they can see billionaires squandering millions on luxury car collections and empty penthouses. There's a perennial history of the working class organizing against long odds to get some share of the owning class's ill-gotten gains—the central force in those stories being the labor movement.

The historical pattern has been carefully analyzed, including by figures who are thought to be the most capitalist. Take Adam Smith, the great Scottish philosopher often considered to be the father of economics. Smith held that markets are efficient in certain circumstances, but at the beginning of the industrial revolution that would create the modern capitalism of today, he already observed the power dynamics at play in the market:

> Masters are always and everywhere in a sort of tacit, but constant and uniform combination, not to raise the wages of labour ... Such combinations, however, are frequently resisted by a contrary defensive combination of the workmen ... It is not, however, difficult to foresee which of the two parties must, upon all ordinary occasions, have the advantage in the dispute, and force the others into a compliance with their terms. The masters, being fewer in number, can combine much more easily; and the law, besides, authorizes, or at least does not prohibit their combinations, while it prohibits those of the workmen.[47]

Other figures, less associated with economics proper but celebrated for their perceptiveness and wisdom, reached similar conclusions. Frederick Douglass, the escaped slave and self-taught intellectual, had this to say about the industrial capitalism roaring up after the Civil War:

> Experience demonstrates that there may be a slavery of wages only a little less galling and crushing in its effects than chattel slavery, and that this slavery of wages must go down with the other ... [T]hose who would reproach us should remember that it is hard for labor, however fortunately and favorably surrounded, to cope with the tremendous power of capital in any contest for higher wages or improved condition.[48]

Martin Luther King Jr., the great civil rights leader, described a similar view of capitalism and class conflict in the twentieth century, and explained the enduring appeal of labor unions to give an

organized workforce some countervailing power against the owning class:

> The labor movement was the principal force that trans-
> formed misery and despair into hope and progress. Out of
> its bold struggles, economic and social reform gave birth to
> unemployment insurance, old-age pensions, government
> relief for the destitute, and, above all, new wage levels that
> meant not mere survival but a tolerable life. The captains of
> industry did not lead this transformation; they resisted it
> until they were overcome . . . [The worker] was hired and
> fired by economic despots whose power over him decreed
> his life or death.[49]

That's the reason for the enduring popularity of the labor
movement, and why it's ruthlessly opposed by business and the ruling class—it's the main weapon, historically and today, for scrap-
ing a share of the national pie from the clutches of the elite. And
especially in their ability to strike, to refuse to labor and turn the
wheels of society without proper compensation, unions reflect too
an understanding that while our property laws give capitalists the
final say over what happens in our society, in fact it is the working
class that holds the ultimate economic power. Without the workers,
no plant can run and no food can be grown, as strikes prove. But
without the CEO, the plant can absolutely still run. It is the working class that holds the real power, and only the social structure of
enforcement of property rights can conceal that.

Modern unions have plenty of problems, but the movement
is going through a real renaissance, as we'll see in chapter 7. Yet
unions have been in brutal decline over the neoliberal period, with
"union density"—the part of the labor force represented by a collective bargaining agreement—falling to 10.1 percent in 2022 after
peaking at over a third in the 1950s, according to the Bureau of
Labor Statistics.[50] In just the private sector, the rate is 6.2 percent.[51]

The beating down of unions, even as they remain popular, has taken two forms: outsourcing work overseas when possible and, when stuck with domestic workers, breaking their unions. Even *Businessweek* has reported that "heightened corporate power has checked union growth ... [C]ompanies also illegally fire union supporters in 25 percent of all elections."[52]

Ehrenreich adds, "Management uses every means possible to intimidate, isolate, and harass the union's supporters ... [M]anagement-run meetings ... may take place daily in the weeks leading up to an NLRB election ... Harder to resist are the one-on-one and small group get-togethers, where individual workers are grilled about their union allegiance for as many hours as it takes. During one union drive among truck drivers, management confronted workers individually about personal issues like their credit ratings and family responsibilities ... [T]he union drive was defeated."[53]

By far the greatest and darkest account of crushing labor is *Confessions of a Union Buster*, consultant Martin Levitt's book on his years breaking unions to keep workers from getting pay raises, health plans, and vacation time. The book is overpoweringly vile despite Levitt's professed remorse, and must be quoted at length:

> Union busting is a field populated by bullies and built on deceit ... The only way to bust a union is to lie, distort, manipulate, threaten, and always, always attack. The law does not hamper the process ... [A] labor relations consultant ... goes to work creating a climate of terror that inevitably is blamed on the union ... The enemy was the collective spirit ... to be sure it would never blossom into a united work force, the dreaded foe of any corporate tyrant ... My team and I routinely pried into workers' police records, personnel files, credit histories, medical records, and family lives in search of a weakness that we could use to discredit union activists. Once in a while, a worker is impeccable. So some consultants resort to lies. To fell

the sturdiest union supporters in the 1970s, I frequently launched rumors that the targeted worker was gay or was cheating on his wife. It was a very effective technique, particularly in blue-collar towns ... We always called union leaders "bosses," for example, to repel the image of the union as a true worker organization. Meanwhile management was painted as humble, caring, righteous ... [A] common strategy among management lawyers, was to challenge everything ... [I]f [a consultant] could make the union fight drag on long enough, workers would lose faith, lose interest, lose hope ... I began to understand that the success of my plan meant, quite plainly, that management would continue to wield absolute control over its workers—that lust for control is, of course, what moved chief executives to agree to hand over control to us; they swallowed their pride for a few months; then, when we were through, they got us out of the building as fast as they could ... The union doesn't get to come inside. The union gets to talk to the workers only after they've heard eight hours' worth of the other side, sometimes accompanied by threats, sometimes by tears.[54]

Playing dirty is common, including framing the union: "I dispatched a contingent of commandos to scratch up the cars of high-profile pro-company workers and to make threatening phone calls to others," then blame the labor organizers.[55]

The battle for the dignity for labor goes on. For now, let's look at what this system of antagonistic class interests does to our society in the meantime.

The Wrong Side of the Tracks

All class-based societies have several features that distinguish life in the various levels. Access to economic resources is the most obvious one, but another enduring feature of hierarchical societies is class segregation. Whether brought about through religious conviction, state policy, or simple market mechanisms, the very strong historical tendency is for the various classes to become physically separated from each other. This allows the elite to avoid having to view the poor and the toiling working class, which might make them feel uncomfortable; and also keeps the increasingly luxurious insanity of the rich out of sight of the working classes, who might be inspired to redistribute some of that wealth, through labor action or politics.

Past societies, with ruling classes based on nobility or aristocracy, saw elites ruling from remote country mansions or giant impregnable castles, which historians say were always intended more to keep the local people subjugated than to defend against foreign invasions. Other societies, like those with major racial cleavages, would often develop very racially cued segregation systems, such as the postwar United States where for many years the Federal Housing Administration would decline to insure homes in Black neighborhoods and private-sector banks practiced "redlining," a policy of declining to extend residential mortgages in those same communities. These practices are one of the main reasons why Black household wealth is so limited today compared to white households in the US.

These separate and unequal experiences occur throughout economic life, not just at home. In 2015, LAX airport agreed to lease a facility to a private company serving the affluent or celebrities willing to cough up $1,800 to avoid long security lines at the terminals. And just like the *Titanic* was strictly segregated into different classes with metal gates, today's giant cruise ships have lately added new, very fancy and very exclusive separate realms of their gigantic vessels with private elevators and set-aside bars and restaurants, private personal assistants on call, and a separate, faster number for room service. The *New York Times* calls it a "money-based caste system"; a McKinsey consultant says, "Class segregation can create something to which people can aspire."[56]

Robert Frank describes the Yellowstone Club, an elite ski resort founded by a rich couple, where "members can ski more than 50 trails without having to wait in lift lines or dodge the hoi polloi . . . Legions of club staff are always on hand to prewarm the members' ski boots, stock their homes with groceries and flowers and, in one case, hand-slice special meat for their dogs. Indeed, the big draw of the Yellowstone Club is the comfort of knowing that everyone around you is wealthy."[57]

Steven Gaines observes some of the abrupt geographical class cutoffs of the ultimate capitalist playground, New York City, in his book on the city's high-end real estate market, *The Sky's the Limit*.

> Some delineations of class and status are obvious to the eye—for instance, the abrupt change north of Ninety-sixth Street on Park Avenue, where railroad tracks rise out of the ground and the pristinely kept co-operative doorman buildings of Carnegie Hill suddenly give way to tenements and bodegas. But there are also more muted differences. There is a "better" side of Park Avenue . . . On Central Park West apartments above Eight-second Street are worth $100,000 less per room, for no discernible reason other than being north of an invisible social demarcation that defines "too far uptown." And while Fifth Avenue might be "the best address," if your apartment is on a floor below the "tree line," usually the fourth floor, and your view of the park is blocked by leaves in the summer or bare branches in the winter, yours is a shabby lot compared with the neighbors above you, whose apartments are worth hundreds of thousands of dollars more per floor the higher you go.[58]

And as shown in chapter 4, class segregation is a major part of the emergency plan for rich families. When COVID-19 shut down schools in 2020, black SUVs lined up in front of doorman buildings in the fine neighborhoods of New York and Paris as affluent families prepared to retreat to their country homes, remote ranch properties, or Caribbean superyachts. All very far away from you grubby proles and your breathy germs, segregated away from the better families of society.

That episode was not an anomaly. Media theory professor Douglas Rushkoff, in his book *Survival of the Richest*, describes an alarming meeting he was invited to with a number of billionaires who asked questions about how to endure their expected future of climate disruptions and worker uprisings:

> How long should one plan to be able to survive with no outside help? Should a shelter have its own air supply? . . . Finally, the CEO of a brokerage house explained that he had nearly completed building his own underground bunker system, and asked, "How do I maintain authority over my security force after the event?" . . . They knew armed guards would be required to protect their compounds from raid-ers as well as angry mobs. One had already secured a dozen Navy SEALS to make their way to his compound if he gave them the right cue. But how would he pay the guards once even his crypto was worthless? What would stop the guards from eventually choosing their own leader? The billionaires considered using special combination locks on the food supply that only they knew. Or making guards wear disci-plinary collars of some kind in return for their survival.[59]

In Rushkoff's account, he argued for more prosocial perspec-tives like using their wealth to help the world deal with these is-sues, and to treat their guards as friends now to ensure loyalty later. "They rolled their eyes."

Besides the endless, ugly injustice of economic segregation, there are other effects of this separation that are less immediately obvious. One is that, as with all forms of segregation, putting walls between people (often literally) means you don't see what's on the other side. This means people just decide that things are very good or very bad "over there," depending on their personality. Some rich or professional-managerial class families have stunningly rosy ideas about how poor and working-class people get by, soothing their own consciences with the easy belief that it's not so bad, and if they're really poor they're used to it so it's not so hard for them. Sure, it's based on nothing and is nakedly self-serving, but with class segregation you're never confronted with any evidence to puncture your pleasing illusions.

Others go in the opposite direction. Many middle-class households have a gut-level, overpowering fear of what they imagine to be the nonstop violence and crime of poor cities and neighborhoods. Because class and race often correlate in many societies, as in the US, France, or the Persian Gulf, there's commonly a racial aspect to this, but not at all universally. Again, the barriers of segregation keep people from actually learning about people in other classes, so you're free to project onto them and their communities any soothing fantasy of plenty or wagon-circling fear that you feel like.

A final note on economic segregation is that it's not just geographic, although of course being on one or another "side of the tracks" was and is the classic form, as Gaines describes. But there are others, one being parallel institutions—children of the ruling class, and even higher PMC families, usually avoid increasingly defunded public schools and instead attend private schools and various elite academies. Mills wrote in *The Power Elite* about the crucial importance of elite schooling: "The private schools do perform the task of selecting and training newer members of a national upper stratum . . . It is in 'the next generation,' in the private school, that the tensions between new and old upper classes are relaxed and even resolved . . . As a selection and training place of the upper classes, both old and new, the private school is a unifying influence, a force for the nationalization of the upper classes . . . It is the characterizing point in the upper-class experience."[60]

Obviously, these academies are typically located in the "better" neighborhoods, which casts a long shadow itself. Places like schools or hospitals or ball courts are where different kinds of people can mix and learn about each other, so the fact that they are themselves sorted by wealth really helps seal off any cracks through which you might learn how the other half lives. Whichever half that is.

And, of course, the other modern definitive form of class segregation is not just geographic, or finessed through private institutions, but vertical. The stupendous heights of residential towers in the great cities allow the owning class to really feel "above it all" and to literally look down on the rest of us. Books like Gaines's on elite real estate leave no doubt that part of the "prestige addresses" of big cities is not just the high-end zip code but also the pretty incredible physical heights from which you may live your stinking rich elite life. Thrillingly, you may be able to see to the other side of the tracks, sure, but you usually can't quite make out what goes on. Perfect.

At times class segregation does break down. In the summer of 2023, a large leaky ship packed with desperate migrants and refugees went down overnight in the western Mediterranean, as tragically happens these days as people flee economic despair and climate change. Six hundred and fifty Egyptians, Pakistanis, and Palestinians drowned. A nearby superyacht, the *Mayan Queen IV*, owned by a Mexican silver magnate, was in the area and was ordered to help the recovery operation. The crew spent hours collecting refugees in the dark.[61] The gleaming pleasure ship, usually full of partiers blasting club music, picked up a hundred survivors and ferried them quietly to port. The image is incredible.

This broad outline gives you a quick taste of how people picture class today. While media reliably fixate on the gap between professionals and manual workers, the bottom line is that anyone working for a living is part of the broad working class, and those whose living mainly comes from property portfolios are the owning class. The numerical facts are a tiny and ever-further-away hyper-rich minority, and a stagnating or slowly declining working majority, with that decline more or less painful depending on the country's economic starting point.

When you recognize the incredible changes to the lives of most people that could be achieved through even a relatively modest redistribution of wealth, you can't really avoid concluding that the many many many people, especially kids, who die as a result of the status quo were effectively murdered. The continuation of any political or economic system that consigns people to live far more grindingly poor lives than necessary is a total godless abomination.

Next, we'll return to the subject of the ruling class and examine the reassuring tales we're told to justify them. Quite a few alibis exist for the rich, but none can get them acquitted of presiding over a class system that sentences the working class to hell.

CHAPTER 4

THE LIES

THE RULING CLASS HAS NO ALIBI

Pioneering doesn't pay.
—**Andrew Carnegie**[1]

People charge Mr. Rockefeller with stealing the money he gave to the church ... but he has laid it on the altar and thus sanctified it.
—**Pastor of the Euclid Avenue Baptist Church, Cleveland**[2]

When you bring up the rich, or the idea of a ruling class, there are a couple of positive things about business and wealth that you are 100 percent iron-clad guaranteed to hear. These lines of argument are abjectly predictable, yet people raising them reliably believe they are brilliant freethinkers who are blowing your mind with their galaxy-brain insights.

In fact, every era and ruling regime has its ideology, a set of socially encouraged beliefs about how society should work, who should be in charge, and what the relationships are between different people. Ideology may come in the form of blatant state propaganda, a party line you're expected to at least pretend to believe, or else. But it can also be a lot more subtle, like an idea or phrase that's so reliably repeated that you come to accept it as "common sense" even without a gun to your head.

But a lie's a lie, and brothers and sisters, we've been living with some doozies. Time to blow away the fog of propaganda and have a look at the man behind the curtain.

Taking a Living

Make a criticism of business, capitalism, or the rich, and some helpful interlocutor will suggest you should be grateful to the ruling class for providing you with a job. "Job creator" is an honored title in the US, bringing with it the suggestion that were it not for your boss hiring you, or some person with money putting their hard-earned cash into a business, then where would you be? Struggling to stay alive catching fish in the creek by hand in your reeking skunk-skin loincloth getting attacked by bears, that's where.

The problem with this particular argument should be clear from chapters 1 and 3 of this book. Throughout history, whatever economic wealth is around has been controlled by the ruling elements of society—state, church, whatever. Agriculturally productive land, valuable slaves, important trade routes, relevant raw materials, all belonged to nobles, kings, churches, or merchants, putting everyone else in a position of inevitable economic dependence. This certainly continues with capitalism today; as readers will know from previous chapters, today's wealth is highly concentrated in the richest households, including the productive economic assets. From large farming estates to plastics factories to oil refineries to power plants to banks, all are private property mostly belonging to giant corporations which themselves are mostly the property of the top households, which own their stock.

As we've seen, this is why the rest of us are members of the working class, regardless of exactly how rough or cushy our particular jobs are. We have no choice but to work for money to pay for necessities, and since nearly all of society's productive wealth is concentrated in so few hands, this obligation means renting yourself to the ruling class's corporate property—getting a job.

So to celebrate the most loaded households by calling them job creators is pretty rich. If anything, they are job hoarders—it is they who can decide who will work the land, where on Earth factories will be located, and what terms you must accept if you want a bank loan to start your own business. They may claim "the market" makes these decisions, and there is some truth to that, but as explored elsewhere today's markets are hyperconcentrated, with only a few giant firms dominating most of them, a condition called "oligopoly." Full monopolies themselves are common too, from patented pharmaceuticals to utilities to network-based monopolies like Google's YouTube.[3] Monopolies aren't quite as common as during the Gilded Age of the late 1800s, before antitrust regulation limited them, but they've made a major comeback since these regulations were themselves dialed back.[4]

We should note too that capitalists are quite proud of their job-*destroying*—of the market economy's drive to find new, cheaper ways of making products, poorer places to move production to, and new technologies to replace workers with. This does indeed mean more efficient production of goods relative to cost, but it also means millions of families can find their livelihoods yanked away overnight. The loss of US manufacturing and the descent of formerly industrial cities into stagnation, unemployment, and drug abuse has taught the American worker one thing: they are considered expendable.

Being in possession of the productive economic assets, or the "means of production" as critical economists say, puts the rich and their CEO representatives in the driver's seat of the economy, above all in the dominant sectors of finance and tech. And for all their claims of great investment risk, as business writers have observed, entrepreneurs "are actually moderate risk takers when their leverage is set against the scale of their wealth."[5]

As is often the case, people making libertarian arguments are really just celebrating the powerful in society and deserve no more credit than the intellectuals who defended past ugly systems of class power, from feudalism to the slave economy to fascism. And as we'll see in the next section, conservatives especially have a tradition of celebrating these people not just for their alleged job creating but for being superior to the average person in general.

The Best Families

Defenders of ruling elites have seldom been satisfied with the argument that the rich deserve their wealth because of their grudging willingness to provide jobs for everyone else. Very commonly, the tendency is to celebrate the rich and powerful as being different *kinds of people* from the rest of us—suggesting that they built their gigantic companies up from scratch by their own almost miraculously superior knowledge, relentless drive, and willingness to make tough calls.

The works of Herbert Spencer, for example, were the Bible of the Gilded Age millionaire industrialists and financiers. Sometimes called the Marx of the rich, Spencer claimed to extend to society the scientific insights of Charles Darwin, whose theory of evolution through processes of natural selection had revolutionized biology. Darwin claimed that competition by organisms for the scarce resources of survival meant the preferential reproduction of organisms well suited to their natural environment, leading to the incredible variety of adaptations to every niche in the living world today.

Spencer claimed to apply this watershed insight to social analysis. But rather than organisms evolving by passing on traits suited to changing ecosystems, Spencer claimed in the competitive economy human individuals also had to fight for scarce resources, and those who became rich were the best-suited to life. And not just best-suited, it also turned out the rich were better *people* too, why just look at their elegant estates and their many luxurious possessions and their fine diction.

Andrew Carnegie, the great Gilded Age steel monopolist, wrote, "While the law [of natural selection] may be sometimes hard for the individual, it is best for the race, because it insures the survival of the fittest in every department," although he frankly admitted capitalism was creating "rigid castes" and called the wealth gap "the problem of our age."[6] Danny Dorling draws out the unflattering implications of these views in *Inequality and the 1%*: "It is remarkable . . . to have to acknowledge that some people really do believe that some of us are actually of 'better stock' than others. They don't say this out loud, of course. Animal breeding metaphors are hardly acceptable as a way to talk about fellow citizens."[7]

More concretely, a paper for the Peterson Institute for International Economics found that while "the superrich in the United States are more dynamic than in Europe," still "just over half of European billionaires inherited their fortunes, as compared to one-third in the United States."[8] That's still a lot of inheritance going on, and for billions of dollars of wealth that are desperately needed by so many people.

But what research we have does not suggest the rich are superior to us, and in fact their wealth-drenched lives seem to lead in the opposite direction. There is a common, and institutionally encouraged pattern of carefully hoarding wealth and keeping it within the family, and putting personal relationships, even marriage, beneath economic imperatives.

The heiress Abigail Disney wrote for the *Atlantic* about her inheritance and how she was "Taught From a Young Age to Protect My Dynastic Wealth," especially once she came into the money at the age of twenty-one. She was "taught certain precepts as though they are gospel: Never spend the 'corpus' (also known as the capital) you were left. Steward your assets to leave even more to your children, and then teach them to do the same. And finally, use every tool at your disposal within the law" to keep the money from the government, which will only waste it on health care for poor people. She also learned to "marry people 'of your own class' to save yourself the complexity and conflict that come with a broad gulf in income, assets, and, therefore, power."[9] She adds, "Having money—a lot of money—is very, very nice . . . I have wallowed in the less concrete privileges that come with a trust fund, such as time, control, security, attention, power, and choice."

And more specifically, we can turn to the body of rigorous social science research on the rich, which tends to reveal that they are assholes. A group of psychologists at the University of California conducted an impressive series of lab and field tests to probe the moral fiber of wealthier people and published the results in the highly prestigious *Proceedings of the National Academy of Sciences*. They found "upper-class individuals behave more unethically than lower-class individuals," being in particular "more likely to break the law while driving, relative to lower-class individuals," and in the lab "were more likely to exhibit unethical decision-making tendencies," as well as to lie, cheat, and take goods from others.[10] The first two studies involved assessing the class signals of oncoming cars at a California traffic intersection, and recording whether the driver obeyed traffic laws and allowed a waiting car to pass or instead cut them off. The second study replaced the second car with a pedestrian, with both studies finding that after controlling for other factors like sex, age, traffic conditions, and the time of day, "upper-class drivers were the most likely to cut off other vehicles" and "were significantly more likely to drive through the crosswalk without yielding to the waiting pedestrian."

In the lab, participants were given a survey to state their subjective view of their personal social and economic standing, and given a well-established exercise to heighten class feeling, by comparing themselves to people with more or less money, education, and better or worse jobs. They then participated in simple lab activities to gauge behavior—being offered candy from a jar that the subject is told will later be given to a room full of children, meaning the more the subject takes, the less remains for kids. Richer subjects took more candy than lower-ranked subjects. Asked to privately roll a die and told the highest-total roller would receive a cash prize, upper-class subjects were more likely to lie to the experimenter and report a higher total roll (all rolls were predetermined to sum up to twelve).

The psychologists then ask rhetorically, "Is society's nobility in fact its most noble actors?" You can guess their conclusion. They chalk up the shitty behavior of the rich to their increased independence, both from economic need and from regard for others' opinions, as well as having the resources to cope with any costs of their unethical behavior.

You can be high-class and pretty classless.

Atlas Ran

Many defenders of capitalism get there through the work of Ayn Rand, a twentieth-century successor to Spencer and author of smash hit libertarian books like *The Fountainhead* and *Atlas Shrugged*. Her very, very, very long novels are thinly veiled libertarian critiques of the more regulated, tax-the-rich capitalism of the New Deal era in which she lived. Rand's books are Spencer pitched at a comic book level—the company executives run the business, invent the actual products themselves, and work long hours to almost single-handedly build their business empires. They are also portrayed in the books as being very hot, and have cool affairs with edgy sex.

Of course, in reality, when we say a CEO "built the company," we know the building was put up by construction workers, the goods it produces are made by factory workers, and the company is run by office workers. In some of the novels, workers demand regulations or more money, and they are depicted as *not* sexy, but fat and gross! The libertarian economist Ludwig von Mises wrote to Ayn Rand, "You have the courage to tell the masses . . . you are inferior and all the improvement in your conditions which you simply take for granted you owe to the effort of men who are better than you."[11] The Randian picture is a race of capitalist supermen, who are creative geniuses who above all *take the risks.*

In the developed world, it's easy to become reasonably comfortable and imagine yourself as owing your plush surrounds to your previous bold gambles of fortune. But in real life, risk and peril are *scary*, no longer an abstract idea but a real risk to yourself. So of course, when it came down to it and the shit hit the fan, the rich hit the road.

The *New York Times* ran an unusually salty 2020 headline, "The Rich Have a Coronavirus Cure: Escape From New York," finding "Broad-scale emergencies never fail to reveal the fault lines in the American class system, and it was suddenly clear that well-off New Yorkers . . . had a powerful inoculant: secondary real estate."[12] The New York press reported heavily on the rich pouring out: "The flight from New York was on. For those who could afford it—like the rich who fled plague-stricken Florence in *The Decameron*—salvation, it seemed, might be reached by the Long Island Expressway. Or at least space, and possibly social distance from their social inferiors. Doorman buildings all over New York had SUVs lined up out front, lifeboats against an invisible virus."[13]

Indeed, an analysis of smartphone data found that the whole city's population fell by about 5 percent, over 400,000 people, over those months. And using census tract data, the pattern was clear: "The higher-earning a neighborhood, the more likely it is to have emptied out."[14] In more tony neighborhoods like the Upper East Side, West Village, and SoHo, the resident population fell by over 40 percent, even as other more middle- and working-class neighborhoods saw much smaller changes.

Bloomberg News then memorably ran the headline "Quandary for High Flyers: How to Travel Safely to Your Yacht," with the riddle: "A yacht awaits at harbor, but how to safely reach it without risking contact with the COVID-exposed masses?"[15] But an enterprising firm, "spurred by member demand," began offering private, pre-sanitized flights to Malta, the popular elite destination with zero income and estate tax, and where citizenship can be openly purchased for $1.3 million American. Once there, a "pre-sanitized car" bears clients to their pre-stocked yachts. The firm notes its Bombardier Global 6000 rents at around $16,000 an hour, plus fees for the "jet-to-yacht service."

The obliviously selfish rich partying during a dangerous epidemic scandalized and delighted the public when it regularly surfaced, often via celebrity news. Nick Bilton thus reported for *Vanity Fair* on a Silicon Valley source grousing that "all these rich people can't stop themselves . . . They just can't stop themselves from throwing parties and going on their jets and socializing as if everything was normal." He recounted,

> countless billionaires hitting the road, flying around the country to wherever case numbers are lowest. One investor worth several billion who has several homes told a friend—who then parlayed the information to me in tones of shock and awe and more than a tinge of jealousy—that he was in Miami when the numbers were lowest at the start of the pandemic; hopped over to Los Angeles when Florida got a bit dicey; and now that California is a hotbed, is in New York enjoying the season's outdoor dining. Another billionaire in Los Angeles has been hosting lavish dinner parties (no social media allowed) where an on-site nurse administers 15-minute coronavirus tests outside as guests drink cocktails, and allows them in to dine once their tests come back negative.[16]

More seriously, the *Guardian* reported the rich "are understood to be taking personal doctors or nurses on their flights to treat them and their families in the event that they become infected. The wealthy are also besieging doctors in private clinics . . . demanding private coronavirus tests."[17] And of course in decamping, the rich and their staff often spread COVID. A small-town Hamptons volunteer firefighter and construction worker told the press, "I don't fault them. They own property; they have a right to be here. But it was definitely brought out here from them."[18]

Throughout the pandemic there was no more sought-after asset than access to medical care. Many of us got familiar with clumsy telemedicine appointments over the COVID years, but the rich had a totally different experience. We're talking about "concierge care . . . typically not covered by insurance, gets around restrictions placed on doctors . . . But it comes at a steep cost: Prices for services can be two to three times higher, and that comes on top of annual fees."[19] In the earliest days of the sickness before mass-produced consumer tests, you could pay $1,000 for a twelve-hour result (plus another $1,000 to have the medical pro come to the Hamptons). A high-end office call from a dermatologist charged a $5,000 fee, transit included, typically by helicopter. Even dentists leaned into elite home appointments, charging "$1,000 for the doctor to walk in the door, $500 for a cleaning and $600 for a whitening, up from $200 in the office."

Chapter 3 described the class segregation typical of historical societies and capitalism today. Ruling elites or today's owning class reliably live in expansive conditions of almost comical sumptuousness, and above all in "exclusive" settings—where everyone else around you is from similar economic backgrounds. White-collar and blue-collar neighborhoods are sorted through simple market prices, but the effect is to frequently wall off different walks of life from one another. These patterns, interesting in themselves, take on renewed importance in conditions of social emergency like the pandemic.

Once isolated in their deluxe ranches, posh vacation estates, and British castles, the world's ruling class had to pass the time too. The *New York Times* reports an in-home, deluxe manicure-pedicure cost $125 during COVID, far more than usual, while concierge-style one-on-one coaching and mentoring for kids was $250 for a ninety-minute session.[20] Meanwhile thousands of fundraisers were running on GoFundMe.com for groceries and rent for the working class. Over $100 million was raised on the crowdfunding site in 2020 for everyday expenses, enough for the company to introduce a new fundraising category for monthly bills—rent and groceries.[21]

The business press also reported on the rich hiding out in the outdoors, at huge luxury ranch properties often in the US West. Property owners who paid around $3 million per luxury "cabin" were able to experience those long, long months of the pandemic, which so many of us spent cooped up in stuffy apartments, in large stately homes with dozens of acres. A rich couple comments, "When you're in town, you're stuck in a house—you can basically walk up and down the streets and that's it. We've got our horses here and 2,000 acres to walk around on and ride on—it just seemed like the place to be."[22]

Again, for the working class, quarantine conditions were different indeed. Housing has always been an easy place to observe the wealth gap, but while the rich fled their urban trophy properties to their rural trophy properties, the poor were marooned in their shittier accommodations.

The prominent Indian writer Arundhati Roy related to the *Financial Times* the story of the hasty and punitive lockdown that was sprung on the country, with only hours' warning:

> Many driven out by their employers and landlords, millions of impoverished, hungry, thirsty people, young and old, men, women, children, sick people, blind people, disabled people, with nowhere else to go, with no public transport in sight, began a long march home to their villages. They walked for days . . . Some died on the way. They knew they were going home potentially to slow starvation . . . As they walked, some were beaten brutally and humiliated by the police, who were charged with strictly enforcing the

curfew ... A few days later, worried that the fleeing population would spread the virus to villages, the government
sealed state borders even for walkers. People who had
been walking for days were stopped and forced to return to
camps in the cities they had just been forced to leave.[23]

Beyond the living conditions of the classes under
COVID-19, there's the question of access to testing and treatments for the disease itself. In the early, scarily confusing days
of the epidemic, access to tests was highly sought-after, and like
everything else in a capitalist market-based system, they went to
those who could pay.

Consider Fisher Island, a Miami Beach private island reach-
able only by ferry and "one of the wealthiest places in America."
There residents were able to secure antibody tests for everyone in
the neighborhood, even when the ferry and marina were closed.
The island, where an equity membership costs $250,000, used con-
nections with the University of Miami to secure the tests. But despite all these VIPs jumping the line, a working-class person could
still get tested. If they worked for one of these rich households.
"Home health aides and housekeepers also got tested."[24]

The rich countries themselves became notorious for securing
vaccine stockpiles capable of inoculating far more people than their
own populations, even as poor countries of the developing world
waited for their first shots. Spurred by genuine uncertainty around
vaccine efficacy and a total lack of concern for the world's poor,
the US and UK signed contracts for four times more doses than
they had population, while Canada ordered six times. A researcher
wrote, "The high-income countries have gotten to the front of the
line and cleared the shelves."[25] Few showed any concern for epide-
miologists' pleas to inoculate the most vulnerable populations in
all countries before moving on to less at-risk populations in each
state—instead, the industry and states have largely catered to the
wealthy of the world.

The world went through a hell of a natural disaster in 2020 to 2023, with some signs (and plenty of corporate encouragement) that COVID is hopefully now transitioning to another endemic respiratory bug like the cold or flu. But society is changed for good it seems, with the rich having greatly enlarged their already glaringly inflated share of the economy even as the global majority was traumatized by going through a yearslong calamity with limited government aid and terrible political leadership.

Nick Bilton quotes a doctor who says, "Coronavirus is a poor person's virus. We're seeing it spread in poor neighborhoods, to poor families who must go to work and live in close proximity to each other."[26] Meanwhile the great successes and job creators of our society, celebrated for their bold investment and risk-taking, immediately rushed the exits with all the room, toys, and drugs they could carry. Diseases take a deadly toll on the human race, but being a gigantic rich asshole is less contagious.

Patently Ridiculous

There is no word more often used to defend the ruling class than "innovation." Arising as a common defense of the rich in the 1990s alongside the popularization of the Internet, the claim is that rich tech CEOs *earned* their private jets and million-dollar watches because they invented useful services like Google, fun devices like the iPhone, and especially the greatest of modern innovations, the Internet itself.

Regrettably, every part of this claim is 100 percent horseshit. Google search, Wi-Fi functionality, and their underlying technologies of radio and the Internet were without exception developed by the state, specifically military research agencies and the university system. The facts of the development of each of these technologies are well established and run in the opposite direction of the claims of allegedly innovative billionaires, but my god are they casually, universally, and unbelievably assumed to be true.

The ruling class and their corporate media property love to talk about innovation and will often deploy its fruits promptly in their operations, if conditions are right. But you can be sure that companies will do so, without fail, in the most controlling and profit-making manner, regardless of the technology's broader potential. And not infrequently, companies have full-on suppressed innovations if they feared they could hurt their existing profit centers. Yet the media fawn over tech CEOs as if they single-handedly invented their key technologies, going so far as to hold up real imbeciles— like the prominent South African mining heir, Tesla-buyer, and Twitter-ruiner Elon Musk—as real-life versions of supergeniuses like Iron Man. It's dumb.

Why wouldn't companies and their wealthy owners support innovation and research into new technologies? The reality of the scientific process is that research is uncertain—you never know if your science staff is on the verge of a new trillion-dollar breakthrough, or instead slogging away at basic research that will never yield a marketable product, let alone a highly profitable one. It can take many years for a research program to yield useful technology, if it ever does, and the problem is that companies are under short-term pressure to meet their profit-per-share targets.

For that reason, basic research and development is most commonly done by public institutions, such as universities and militaries, which are mostly immune to near-term profitability goals. Since research takes a long time, is uncertain of any payoff, and is also frequently quite expensive, it's not reasonable (at least within market logic) to expect private firms to pour resources into costly R&D that may never pay off. But public institutions can do this, and as a result most major technological developments have taken place within that sector.

Consider the Internet. Most of us use it via Wi-Fi, the short-range radio signal system that allows your phone to download your email, post cat videos, and view pornography. Radio as a usable wireless communication system was famously developed by

Guglielmo Marconi, for the Italian navy. Wi-Fi itself was developed by the University of Hawaii in the 1970s to manage access to its one mainframe in Honolulu for its dispersed network of island campus computers. Named ALOHAnet, the one-way radio signals would in time form the basis for modern Wi-Fi standards.[27]

The Internet itself was originally known as ARPANET, named for ARPA, the Advanced Research Project Agency, the Pentagon's main research arm. The development of this technology took decades, during which the military, select research universities like MIT and Stanford, and the National Science Foundation spent major resources for a dispersed communication system that could perhaps survive nuclear war, manage the military's sprawling Cold War surveillance system, and help scientists share datasets.

The government research agencies even tried a few times to get the private sector interested in the potential of the technology and to take over the research—the United States has a strong tendency to privatize public assets. But again and again, companies from IBM to AT&T flatly declined to take over managing the new inter-network.[28] ARPA and the universities developed the crucial tech, like packet-switching and certain universal technical standards so that different networks could communicate with one another, culminating in the first successful test in 1977.

Of course, the Internet itself was only of limited use until the advent of the World Wide Web, using the HTML technical standards developed by UK physicist Tim Berners-Lee, who built them to create an operations tool for a public research facility, the European Laboratory for Particle Physics at CERN in France and Switzerland.[29] This technical standard allowed for the use of the Internet to exchange data constituting Web pages, along with email (then the main form of Internet use, prior to the development of mobile telephony and apps in the 2000s). Berners-Lee developed the standards and released them publicly for free, allowing them to be used by the decentralized body of Internet users, rather than keeping them as trade secrets with proprietary protocols that were incompatible with any other users, which the main computing companies like IBM and Apple preferred to do.

Eventually, the now-proven Internet architecture was finally privatized by the Clinton administration in the 1996 Telecommunications Act. It was only then that firms saw enough commercial potential in the online network, building up early dial-up-era portals like AOL. Without the decades of public funding of the Internet, it would have remained undeveloped and all the value created by Amazon, Google, and smartphones could never have been realized (for better or worse).

And even these online platforms themselves required significant public support to get through their money-losing stages and reach profitability. Google's first web address, after all, was not google.com but google.stanford.edu, since it was developed in a research lab by grad students with public funding from the National Science Foundation.[30]

Reputation Laundering

No defense of the powerful is more universal than celebrating their good works of generosity. Far older than capitalism, this line of thinking has been used to defend the powerful throughout history, from kings to popes to CEOs. Sure, the king may oppress us with taxes for his own comforts, and draft us to fight his crusades, and appoint violent inbred imbecile lords to rule over the fief we live in, but he gives a few shillings to the Sisters of Benevolence Hospice for the Dying. So let's stop criticizing him and focus on those evil Muslim Turks!

An old argument indeed. But of course, no matter how much the town criers may be required to sing the praises of the powerful when they feel like conspicuously dropping a few crumbs down to our level, you can't justify power by occasional good deeds, whether heartfelt or merely made as tactical moves to mollify restless subjects. No one wants a king even if he's nice. Maybe he has a kid die suddenly or has a stroke, and becomes less nice, or dies himself and gets replaced by a less-friendly relative. Concentrated power like that has historically been seen as antagonistic to freedom, since power can dictate to you and limit your liberty.

But many people must have failed to get the message, because philanthropy remains a major way for powerful people to try and essentially launder their dirty reputations by using some of their ill-gotten gains to put up a library or orphanage or soup kitchen for regular people. It is completely ubiquitous among the rich today to put some modest slice of the family wealth into a well-publicized bequest to a university or hospital and expect endless praise as well as their name on the building.

A Wyoming mutual fund manager quoted by Freeland in *Plutocrats* even sips his own Kool-Aid. He states, "People don't realize how wealthy people self-tax . . . You know, there's a fellow who was the CEO of Target. In Phoenix, he's created a museum of music. He put in around $200 million of his own money. I have another friend who gave $400 million to a health facility in Nebraska or South Dakota, or someplace like that . . . I think we should get rid of taxes as much as we can . . . Because you get to decide how you spend your money, rather than the government."[31]

Note that if there were real commitment to solving humanity's problems, the money is genuinely there. UN World Food Programme head David Beasley perhaps unwittingly proved how insincere this Spirit of Giving among the wealthy truly is when he noted that a single one time donation of $2 billion would be adequate to eliminate world hunger, and that the figure was only about 2 percent of the net worth of Elon Musk at that time.[32] Warren Buffett did give each of his kids a $10 million charitable foundation "as a Christmas present at the end of the 1990s,"[33] but no billionaire has yet offered Beasley the funds to wipe out hunger. The specific number cited has been questioned as too small, but even five times that amount would equal less than 10 percent of Musk's fortune at the time. So while the ruling class is truly in collective possession of the means to cure many of the world's painful ills, it dispenses crumbs at a time and issues a professional press release with each tiny morsel.

Business reporter Robert Frank recognizes that many rich "view charity as a cheap way to burnish their image. Others simply want to buy their way into society."[34] Yet, like his colleagues, he also breathlessly celebrates a finance millionaire who's sick of Big Charity and runs his own "entrepreneurial charity," just like a business! His charity, which is seriously called A Glimmer of Hope, "has performance targets built into every grant he makes. When he funds a small NGO in Ethiopia, he pays it only for the first quarter. If it achieves its goals—digging a certain number of wells, or starting a school—he funds the NGO a second quarter. If it doesn't, it loses the funding. At first, the Ethiopian NGOs resented the process. They saw it as overly demanding and punitive... Now, he says, most of the groups are used to it. 'These developing nations have become dependent on handouts,' he says. 'Grants became an entitlement.'" His business card reads "Philip Berber—Glimmer of Hope."[35]

Sociologist Linsey McGoey reports on this trend of "philanthrocapitalism," where charity "emulates the way business is done in the for-profit capitalist world" and "describes a way that capitalism itself can be naturally philanthropic, driving innovation." The problem, she observes, is that this partial provisioning of services undermines support for public services from the government that are available to everybody. Worse, "many philanthropists... earned their fortunes through business strategies that greatly exacerbate the same social and economic inequalities that philanthropists purport to remedy."[36]

Andrew Carnegie is probably the most famous ruling-class philanthropist, with Carnegie libraries in over three hundred US cities, and many museums funded by him. Generous indeed, but the money came from one of the really great evil Gilded Age monopolies. Carnegie's empire of steel plants is described in John

Kampfner's incredible book *The Rich*: "He squeezed the maximum production out of his workforce . . . In his steel mills, the workers worked twelve-hour days, doing a whole twenty-four hours on alternate Sundays, irrespective of the prospect of accidents—just so they would be allowed to take the following Sunday off. For Carnegie and his generation of investors and industrialists sitting in their plush offices, the money kept rolling in."[37]

Carnegie's rival, the great oil monopolist John Rockefeller, controlled an almost incomprehensible amount of wealth in the later 1800s, and as he therefore became subject to increasing public suspicion, he began making large, headline-grabbing donations. Rockefeller gave $600,000 (over $20 million in today's money) to the University of Chicago, leading it to develop its economics department which then and now is distinguished in its support of the gigantic monopolistic trusts such as the one Rockefeller operated; one economics professor criticized the railroad cartels and was fired by the university for "incompetence."[38]

Since then, the University of Chicago economics department has become famous as one of the most conservative and pro-market schools in the world, indeed has played an active role in undermining rare socialist governments around the world. When Rockefeller gave a further three million to the school, students are said to have sung:

John D. Rockefeller
Wonderful man is he
Gives all his spare change
To the U. of C.
He keeps the ball a-rolling
In our great varsity[39]

But Bill Gates, the Rockefeller admirer, Microsoft cofounder, and one of the world's richest men, is probably the modern definitive case. Gates is now considered by many people to be one of the better billionaires when compared to Donald Trump or the Koch brothers. This is mainly due to the Bill & Melinda Gates Foundation being the world's largest private charitable entity, with billions in its endowment, used for fighting AIDS, accelerating economic development, and many other worthy causes.

Gates's fortune comes from Microsoft, which for decades had a global computer operating system monopoly. During his company's manic growth period, Gates emerged as a modern Gilded Age tycoon. Even sympathetic biographers refer to Gates's frequent "abrasive, childish rants" and "childlike temper tantrums."[40] More importantly, Gates was a dedicated monopolist from the very earliest days. "We're going to put Digital Research out of business," a standard history book of the company recounts him saying, "slamming his fist into the palm of his other hand. He would issue a similar vow twice more during the next year . . . promising to put MicroPro and Lotus out of business, each time emphasizing his promise by smashing his fist into his hand."[41]

The near fanatical pursuit of this cause led to Microsoft's famous '90s-era antitrust case, which it eventually lost with the company being legally declared a monopolist. Gates turned out to have lied extensively in his video deposition for the case, and came to be seen as such a condescending robber baron that he literally became a Simpsons villain.[42]

It was during this time when Gates's reputation was in the toilet that he discovered charitable giving. It took no time at all for the popular press to begin falling over itself to celebrate Gates's generosity, with *Wired* gushing that his foundation had "saved some 6 million lives," and created "a new era in philanthropy, in which decisions—often referred to as investments—are made with the strategic precision demanded of business and government, then painstakingly tracked to gauge their success."[43]

The business press sums up the effect: "Twenty years ago, people associated the name Gates with 'ruthless, predatory' monopolistic conduct." However, "after taking a public relations beating during [the Microsoft antitrust] trial's early going in late 1998, the company started what was described at the time as a 'charm offensive' aimed at improving its image ... Mr. Gates contributed $20.3 billion, or 71 percent of his total contributions to the foundation ... during the 18 months between the start of the trial and the verdict."[44] A wealth manager frankly states, "His philanthropy has helped 'rebrand' his name."

But even here we see the limits of meeting social needs through rich-people philanthropy. The Gateses' divorce has put into question how the Foundation may change its priorities, a monumentally important question because it funds so many projects. And indeed Melinda French Gates "is no longer pledging to give the bulk of her wealth to the Bill & Melinda Gates Foundation and instead plans to spread it among philanthropic endeavors," and as she put it: "I recognize the absurdity of so much wealth being concentrated in the hands of one person, and I believe the only responsible thing to do with a fortune this size is give it away—as thoughtfully and impactfully as possible."[45] On her terms, on her timetable, and aligned with her own shifting priorities.

And in this era of tax cuts for wealthy households and the resulting government budget deficits, many advocates of cutting back the social safety net still point to private philanthropy and "faith-based" organizations as potential substitutes. But this is immediately ludicrous. Private charities, even on the scale reviewed here, are nowhere near capable of paying for a country's social needs—whether that need is housing the mentally ill or providing vaccines.

The foundations themselves recognize this, as when Patty Stonesifer, then chief of the Gates Foundation, admitted, "Our giving is a drop in the bucket compared to the government's responsibility."[46] This was further confirmed when the Foundation committed $50 million to fight the 2014 West African Ebola outbreak, while the UN estimated the total cost of containing the epidemic at roughly $600 million.[47] Definitely within the reach of these modern foundations, but far beyond the kind of commitment they are known to make. Hell! Since its founding, the Gates Foundation has had a yearly health budget larger than the UN's World Health Organization.[48]

Further, the rich are themselves bad sources of ongoing philanthropic commitment, because they're so fickle. Michael Bloomberg, the great media monopolist and billionaire, wrote, "I'd argue another gift to fight a disease that has a lot of the world's attention and people are focusing on it is not where I want us to go." A related *Forbes* headline read that Bloomberg is "Bored of Philanthropy."[49] The late real estate kingpin, Leona Helmsley, left $12 million to her dog, Trouble, and billions more for causes supporting the welfare of dogs. The press reports on her estate: "The first goal was to help indigent people, the second to provide for care and welfare of dogs. A year later . . . she deleted the first goal."[50]

This giving is all transparently cosmetic, too. When the roof of the great Parisian cathedral Notre Dame tragically burned down in 2019, rich Frenchmen were one-upping each other on how much they pledged toward the repair and reconstruction. A 100-million euro donation from the second-richest Frenchman was followed literally hours later by a 200-million euro donation from the richest one. Soon nearly a billion euros had been pledged by rich French families and corporations, yet a second inferno was ignited when an adviser to one of the French billionaires posted online that such donations should receive a 90 percent tax deduction rather than the normal 60 percent.[51] For a country already convulsed with demonstrations by a movement against regressive taxes (see chapter 5), this led to furious demands for reinstatement of the wealth tax recently abolished by the neoliberal French government. The adviser withdrew the suggestion. More broadly, billionaire Eli Broad spelled out the goal of giving when he said, "I'm not aware of any large gifts that are anonymous," and indeed an Indiana University survey found a mere 1 percent of million-dollar-plus gifts are given anonymously.[52] The stupidly wealthy want everyone to know how generous they are.

Even worse, rich philanthropists are often incompetent, thinking they're above traditional development entities and end up exacerbating the problems they claim to be trying to solve, or creating entirely new ones. A great example comes again from the Gates Foundation, which makes a major part of its branding a special commitment to the eradication of malaria in the developing world. The classic means of doing this, among many charitable entities, is the distribution of mosquito nets—synthetic nets with tiny holes, allowing air to circulate during sleep but too small for the disease-spreading pests to get through. Many mosquito nets are further coated in pesticides.

But the large charities failed to consider the realities of desperate poverty, where rather than use the nets to keep away malaria while sleeping, the poor repurpose them for fishing. In south-central Africa, the nets are stronger than traditional woven nets, and used to scoop up whole swaths of lake and coastal sea bottoms, dragging up very small fish that would escape normal fishing nets. But this also includes the juvenile fish fry needed to reproduce the next generation of adult fish, and, further, the fact that the nets are covered in pesticides often means that they have poisoned the small ponds and precious regional lakes in the region. Hundreds of millions of these nets are passed out for free to the poor of Africa and the developing world every year, many labeled "Do not wash in a lake or a river."[53] Some become chicken coops and even bridal veils.

And even if we set aside all this, there is still the fact that when things go badly wrong for the rich, all of their generous donations can disappear. The failed cryptocurrency exchange platform FTX and its disgraced founder Sam Bankman-Fried made extensive contributions to charitable entities before the market predictably crashed and extensive wild misuse of depositor money was discovered. FTX, now in bankruptcy court receivership, began trying to claw back much of the money, with a number of tech and media nonprofits having to return over a million dollars apiece donated by the company or Bankman-Fried's family foundation. Bankman-Fried himself told the press that "the majority of his charitable giving was sincere. But he also said that some was to curry favor with the public. 'When I pledged to give away $2,000 to some brand name charity as part of some promotion related to FTX's business, that was as much PR as anything else.'"[54]

Similarly, McGoey observes that many foundations welcome "pledges" that may or may not ever materialize. She notes billionaire Richard Branson's 2006 pledge to the Clinton Global Initiative to donate $3 billion to climate change–related causes over the following ten years. He ended up spending $300 million, about one-tenth that amount.[55]

Giving to your local charity and activist groups is great. But high-end philanthropy is uniformly ruling-class reputation laundering, giving away pennies from towering fortunes they should be forced to give up altogether. And when regular people do their philanthropy, it's often much closer to home—the University of Chicago found that fifty million Americans, 20 percent of the country, have contributed to a crowdfunding campaign for medical bills. About half of such donations were for coworkers, and an accompanying survey found that 60 percent of respondents said the government has "a great deal or a lot of responsibility" for providing help when a person can't afford medical care, and another 25 percent said "some responsibility."[56] Instead, we donate $20 to each other when we get sick or hurt while the rich are on TV congratulating themselves for bungling some project in the Third World.

The socialist writer Nathan Robinson read a large pile of books by billionaire entrepreneurs and found that "Billionaires tell themselves many things. They say that market price is value, meaning that if you're making money, you're helping the world. They say that they are rewarded for risk and hard work, even though they don't risk anything of value and people who work far harder than they do earn pittances . . . Their justifications for their success crumble when touched."[57]

All these arguments are so well-worn that defenders of the ruling class will rattle them off with the reliability of a reflex action. Throw shade at any billionaire or trillion-dollar corporation and some dweeb will be making a Brave Defense of Free Enterprise with these exact tired saws. Any socialist should be prepared with these rebuttals and details—hopefully you can pull away the fig leaf from the ruling class's shriveled claims to build up society and soothe its wounds, when it is labor and the Earth's bounty that truly built their wealth.

These weak-sauce alibis may be laughable, but the dominant commercial media, on TV, radio, and online, will repeat them until the end of time because after all they're the *property* of the same owning class and aren't run by people who were hired to criticize the boss. It's a central part of how we're controlled by capitalists even in relatively free republics in the developed world—major media and online platforms can choose the facts you hear and shape your perspective on the world until everyone believes in the same "common sense." But the elite's claims of job creation, innovation, and made-for-TV charity balls aren't going to fool the world forever. Which is good, because as we'll see in the next chapter, the world's clock is ticking.

CHAPTER 5

THE BURDEN

WHAT ABOUT THE CLIMATE?

[T]here is scarcely any limit to the carbon emissions of the ultra-wealthy.
—**World Inequality Report**[1]

I owe the public nothing.
—**J. P. Morgan**,[2] after the Panic of 1901

A third of the world's wealth is in the hands of its richest one percent, including ownership of the productive economy through financial assets. A class that thinks of itself as having superior individual characteristics like risk tolerance actually spends its existence decked out in purposeless excess, pouring resources into their toys on a mind-boggling scale.

But we're not done with the parade of hilarious disgrace yet, because the owning class of our weary world is also responsible for a surprisingly large share of the damage "we" are doing to the planet itself. Their heavy consumption of material resources across the board, and their concentrated ownership of the global corporate conglomerates responsible for so much of today's environmental pollution, are an important part of any portrait of the ruling class. And as we'll see, their hoard of the world's wealth comes with a giant share of the world's carbon emissions: the top 10 percent of world households emits almost half the greenhouse emissions of the entire world, and the richest 1 percent nearly 17 percent by itself. Besides their own wide-mouthed consumption, their share arises from their ownership of most of the stock in the great industries that consume a staggering share of global energy.[3]

You can see how the numbers get run up. The world now has thousands of superyachts, with features like glass elevators, marble floors, onboard Turkish steam baths, and air-conditioned helicopter hangars.[4] A single one of those superyachts burns over a hundred gallons of diesel an hour standing still, and releases as much yearly greenhouse emissions as eight hundred cars.[5]

All the living organisms of the natural world have no one to count on but us to do something about the absolute overturning of natural systems we have carried out in the blink of an evolutionary eye. Strap in, this horror show has no intermission!

Wealth CO_2ncentration

As long as there has been a modern, capitalist ruling class, it has been the driving force damaging and consuming the environment, and not just with its lopsided levels of consumption and ownership of the productive economy. These people are also most able to insulate themselves from the consequences of their actions through the market force of class segregation, living far from the most destructive and poisonous results of fast-growing economic activity. The rich set fire to the planet, but get to reside in green, environmentally-spared places, essentially paying for fresh air and clean water while the poor of the world, from Pakistan to Detroit, get to consume water laden with lead or poisoned with pesticides.

During California's brutal drought of the 2010s, some wealthy owners of large estates evaded high fees from water utilities, created to encourage conservation during years of bone-dry weather, by simply trucking in water from out of town. TV personality and consumer trends magnate Oprah Winfrey had large trucks with thousands of gallons arrive at the gates of her estate each day. Oprah is said in time to have cleaned up her act, but reports cite the three biggest private, nonagricultural water consumers in California's Santa Barbara County as sucking up thirty million gallons of water between them over 2012–13.[6] Meanwhile, today's increasingly powerful climate change–boosted hurricanes frequently overwhelm water treatment plants and infrastructure in poor, majority-Black cities in the American South. Unable to pay for trucked-in water, low-income households end up boiling tap water for months on end.[7]

Nature and "environmental services" are increasingly privatized, along with everything else in our neoliberal era. Recall from chapter 2 that the "new status symbol for America's uber-rich" is "trophy trees," which involves wealthy homeowners buying mature, attractive trees and having them pulled out by the roots and trucked to their estates. At a cost of up to a quarter million dollars, the trees "have the added bonus of being able to signify the owner's environmental credentials and their passion for sustainability."[8] If something more seasonal is better suited to the taste of the fabulously wealthy, they could take their lead from media kingpin Sumner Redstone, who once had a full ton of snow trucked to his gigantic 123-room mansion so he could enjoy a white Christmas.[9]

The scientific community, which has been pulling its hair out for decades trying to get powerful people to take environmental collapse seriously, has become remarkably critical of the relationship of capitalism to the environment. A paper in the top-level prestigious journal *Nature Communications* reviews a very broad body of literature on the resource-intensity of consumption, the relation of consumption of goods to emissions, and the problem of an economic system with a growth necessity. They find "humanity needs to reassess the role of growth-oriented economies and the pursuit of affluence ... [P]revailing capitalist, growth-driven economic systems have not only increased affluence since World War II, but have led to enormous increases in inequality, financial instability, resources consumption and environmental pressures on vital earth support systems." Resource use is driven by broadly affluent consumers in the developed world and also by "members of powerful factions of the capitalist class." They advocate a range of solutions; some are modest, including "reducing the need for consumption" through "increasing lifespan of goods, telecommunication instead of physical travel, sharing and repairing instead of buying new, and house retrofitting." Others are more radical, up to and including "eco-socialist approaches, viewing the democratic state as an important means to achieve the socio-ecological transformation."[10]

Today the most prominent and pressing environmental question is climate change. Its destructive record and worse potential are driving a great movement to commit real economic resources to fighting it, including proposals like the Green New Deal in the US that would tax the rich to create jobs needed for a major energy industry transition from fossil fuels to green renewables. But conservatives have reliably politicized the issue, for example when the hoary commentator George Will blandly declared, "Global warming is socialism by the backdoor."[11]

But the dangers are monumental. In 2023, days of awful choking smoke haze shrouded New York City and Washington DC, forcing centers of power and media to experience the "smoke season" formerly known as "summer" in California and other western US states. The most recent report by the Intergovernmental Panel on Climate Change, the definitive global scientific body gathering researchers' growing understanding of climate change, found in 2023 that human civilization is definitively causing global climate change, that the effects grow as our fossil fuel emissions continue, and that climatic shifts will hurt food production, water availability, and quality of life for millions and indeed billions of people globally.[12] The poorest parts of the world, centered

in lower latitudes, are most at risk from the changes to climate
and are those who can least afford to adapt to them. Young people above all are increasingly concerned about the uncontrolled
spiraling of the climate and the world environmental situation,
with research documenting their elevated stress and anxiety as
the process unfolds.[13]

The responsibility for climate emissions is usually split up nationally or regionally, with the originators of the Industrial Revolution, the Western realms of Europe and North America, frequently
estimated as responsible for about half of all total historical greenhouse gas emissions between them. China, almost universally
referred to today as the greatest carbon emitter, is a relative new-
comer to modern development and is thus estimated to be responsible for about half of Europe's total, so far.[14] It's widely recognized,
however, that the developing world (or the Third World as Western audiences used to say), has played a tiny role in the historically
rapid release of all these climate-altering emissions, but is climat-
ically and geographically more vulnerable to them than the Western culprits. But, so far the developed countries have succeeded in
economically forcing the developing world into the "emissionary"
position, making a strong case for future climate reparations.

As with other areas, we can find data on the share of emissions by class. And it shouldn't surprise us to find that the rich,
being the biggest owners and spenders of wealth generally in our
society, are to blame for a gigantic share of the climate changes
we will be enduring in the coming decades. Emissions profiles by
household wealth are as lopsided as those of income, which makes
sense because the more you consume, the more energy is used to
make goods for you, and the more assets you own, the more responsibility you share for the economy's emissions. Economists are
quick to celebrate capitalism and its long-term economic growth,
producing more goods and services for us to consume. But beyond the problem that most of those goods and wealth go to the
already-rich, the messy side effects of our economy grow just as

the economy itself grows. The fast growth of these side effects, or "externalities," is often brushed aside by economists even as they celebrate capitalism's huge growth in production and wealth.[15]

The actual data on this chasm of emissions responsibility are pretty brutal, with the most comprehensive research again coming from the World Inequality Database, referred to frequently in chapter 1. The *World Inequality Report 2022* has extensive recent information on the distribution of emissions, just as it does for the distribution of wealth. And notably, it includes territorial emissions from countries but also a credible measure of carbon emitted in national imports, keeping those carbon footprints from being outsourced overseas and off national carbon budgets.

The WID confirms the historical contributions to climate emissions, with 27 percent from the US-Canada and 22 percent from Europe, large shares due to their early industrial revolutions and their dramatic growth in economic production, energy consumption, and thus emissions.[16] As important as that is, the real headline result relates to the contribution not by region, but by class. Noting that "inequalities in average carbon emissions between regions are quite close to the inequality in average incomes between regions," the report finds that globally, "the top 10% emit 31 tonnes [of CO_2-equivalent per person per year] (47.6% of the total). The top 1% emits 110 tonnes (16.8% of the total). Global carbon emissions inequality thus appears to be very great: close to half of all emissions are due to one tenth of the global population, and just one hundredth of the world population (77 million individuals) emits about 50% more than the entire bottom half of the population (3.8 billion individuals)."[17]

Further damaging for the case that the rich have a positive role to play in the transition to green energy, the researchers find that from 1990 to 2019, "the top 1% is responsible for 21% of emissions growth." Meanwhile the global bottom 50 percent was culpable for 16 percent of this growth.[18] This is relevant since further economic growth—increasing the amount of goods and services produced over time—is the universal economic goal of all current political and certainly business leadership. Worse, it's the most popular proposed way of raising the standards of living among the world's poor. Punting the welfare of the poor to future economic growth fails on its own terms, since the giant majority of the gains of growth go the already-rich, but will also consign us to a future of uncontrolled climate change driven hardest by those same elite households.

A final, dark aspect of the WID accounting of emissions inequality is the remaining "carbon budget"—the amount of fossil fuel emissions that can still be released while keeping the world within a limited amount of projected climate change, such as increases in average land temperatures of 1.5°C or 2.0°C. The more climate warming we experience, the more damaging the effects will be, in rising sea levels and summer temperatures, more and worse droughts and floods, and more general weather destabilization. But having already burned so much carbon to develop our capitalist economies, the remaining budget is limited.

The WID researchers observe that only the poorest halves of most regions are within the per capita allowances of the present UN climate targets, and offers the tough conclusion: "It follows that all emissions reductions efforts are to be made by the top half of the distribution. In the US, "the top 10% must cut its emissions by close to 90%," although also "the middle 40% by around 50%."[19]

The report recommends progressive carbon taxes on the highest emitters, to discourage emissions and raise badly needed funds for adaptation. And in a thoughtful note, they point out that such policies help shift focus from consumers to asset owners, since "carbon consumers . . . are often constrained in their energy choices, because they are locked-in carbon intensive infrastructures systems. On the contrary, investors who opt for investments in fossil industries do so while they have many alternative options to invest their wealth in."[20]

The details reflect the shifting class conflict of recent decades. A report for the Paris School of Economics from WID contributors noted, "Global CO_2e emissions remain highly concentrated today: top 10% emitters contribute to about 45% of global emissions, while bottom 50% emitters contribute to 13% of global emissions. Top 10% emitters live on all continents, with one third of them from emerging countries."[21] The detailed contours of emissions inequality are attested in other research, including several impressive reports from Oxfam, the prominent children's charity.[22]

The Paris School report suggests a broadly representative portrait of a top 1 percent–emitting person, reflecting the top emissions profile generally: "A rich American traveling 5 times a year from New York to Los Angeles (round trips, first class) and twice a year to Europe can emit up to $35tCO_2$e per year, solely for her air transport emissions," with another ten-ton equivalent for automobile use, and another ten for home energy in a year. But the final yearly figure for these elite emitters comes to an incredible three hundred tons of CO_2-equivalent, with a giant portion coming from "the production of all the services and goods purchased by the household that given year," the transportation of these goods to the elite consumer, and the emissions associated with their often-enormous investments.[23]

A final class aspect of the climate crisis is well reviewed by Matt Huber, geography professor at Syracuse University, who observes that "industrial capital . . . is responsible for the bulk of emissions in capitalist society." Citing figures from the quite mainstream Energy Information Administration, he observes the industrial sector constituted 54.8 percent of the world's energy use in 2018, relative to residential use at 12.6 percent, transportation use at 25.5 percent, and commercial use at 7 percent. Using IPCC data, he finds the whole residential sector, even with household transportation included, accounts for less than 15 percent of world energy use, despite the constant emphasis in climate media and politics on personal energy use choices.[24]

The relevance of this data for our purposes is of course that the owning class has among its holdings the equity in the world of production and industry, through its ownership of most corporate stock. As seen in chapter 1, the richest 1 percent of US households by wealth owned 40 percent of all stocks in 2016, and the top 10 percent held 84 percent.[25] So the emissions of the enormous capitalist productive economy are part of the owning class's liability as well. If they get to keep the profits from it, they can be responsible for the emissions from it.

Huber adds that the common view that "all of us" are responsible for the climate crisis is better recast as "a small minority of owners who control and profit from the production of the energy, food, materials, and infrastructure society needs to function."[26] For these reasons, Huber called his book *Climate Change as Class War*.

The monumental emissions of the richest people in the world are a fair target for climate rage.

Abetting the Jet Set

In media portrayals, private jets may have pushed aside superyachts as the definitive global elite status signifier, even as they have become more associated with a showy squandering of the world's carbon budget. Conspicuous consumption, long recognized as impressive consumption of resources, can also extend to consumption of the world carbon budget. Industry reports put the average wealth of a private jet owner at approximately $1.5 billion, observing the incredible expense of buying, fueling, and staffing a private aircraft. Sticker prices range from $14 million for a Cessna Citation XLS up to $42 million for a Falcon 2000DX.[27]

Elite events, like the famous Sun Valley Conference in rural Idaho known as "summer camp for billionaires," can see rural airstrips transformed into parking lots for private planes. The interiors are what you'd expect from people able and willing to spend a couple tens of millions of bucks on private transportation. Robert

Frank's description of one private plane in his book *Richistan* gives the flavor: "[The interior had] a handwoven carpet from Thailand, made from wool and silk, with 14 colors, at $600 a yard . . . The cupboards were stocked with Versace china, Christofle silver and Lalique crystal." Not to mention alligator-skin toilet seats.[28] He also notes that "the waiting list for Gulfstreams is now two years long, and some buyers are selling their 'slots' on the Gulfstream waiting list for up to $1 million to more impatient buyers."[29]

Forbes, the flagship magazine for insufferable rich conservative bastards everywhere, recently reviewed a research agency's report on the world profile of private jet owners.[30] A number of interesting findings emerge, including exactly how common their use is among ultra-high-net-worth individuals, those with a net worth over $30 million. Fully 69 percent of private jets are owned in North America, yet despite fast growth, "just" 14.1 percent of UHNWIs own one, whereas in Latin America and the Caribbean, the number of registered jets is 23.4 percent of the UHNWI population. The number of jets per UHNW person is higher in Africa than the US or Europe as well, at 18.8 percent. The magazine notes this "may have more to do with the fact that in North America and Europe, there is a much broader range of options to access private aviation." Popular options like fractional ownership programs, similar to time-share condos for private jets, or "jet cards" for buying bulk time on private craft, are most common in the US and help extend private jet privilege to mere very-high-net-worth individuals.

In a truly stunning report, Swedish management professor Stefan Gössling compiled an incredible profile of private jet use in the *Annals of Tourism Research*. Reacting to the trend of "flight shaming" and reflecting that "little is known about the air travel patterns of affluent and influential people," Gössling developed an innovative method of using social media accounts to develop data on billionaire and celebrity air travel patterns.[31] He notes the context that "household studies have regularly found that higher income groups are also the most mobile," and that emissions from transport and travel account for the largest part of carbon inequality.

Gössling also observes that politicos and celebrities who enjoy being seen as leaders or spokespeople for the legitimate and valuable movement to address climate change are broadly seen as hypocritical phonies: "Al Gore has been repeatedly criticized for his energy-intense lifestyle, including the use of private aircraft"; and noting the opprobrium when "actor Emma Thompson flew from Los Angeles to London to join a protest of the Extinction Rebellion Movement." More evidently earnest figures, like Swedish climate activist Greta Thunberg, have embraced principled non-flying lifestyles.

But the paper's highlight is Gössling's use of Instagram, Twitter, and Facebook posts to construct private flight maps for 2017 for a number of global figures, combined with known purchases or ownership of private aircraft. Gössling recognizes that such posts are curated by the creators, who will likely exempt some trips or stops for security or privacy reasons. Still, the resulting maps are incredible and reproduced in figures 1 and 2.

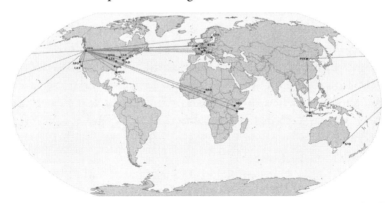

Figure 1. Flight patterns of Bill Gates, 2017. From Stefan Gössling, "Celebrities, Air Travel, and Social Norms," *Annals of Tourism Research* 49, no. 4 (October 2019).

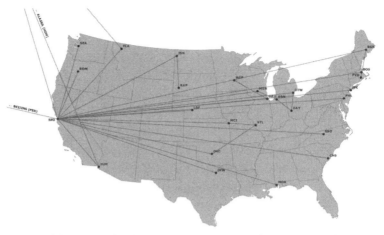

Figure 2. Flight patterns of Mark Zuckerberg, 2017. From Stefan Gössling, "Celebrities, Air Travel, and Social Norms," *Annals of Tourism Research* 49, no. 4 (October 2019).

As you can see, the travel is extensive, especially for a single year and given the near certainty of undercounting. Gössling found "the average flight by Bill Gates, at 5821 km, was about twice as long as the average flight by Jennifer Lopez and four times the average distance flown by Karl Lagerfeld." Noting that total emissions vary significantly, "on the high side of the emissions' [*sic*] spectrum, Bill Gates' flight activity generated >1600 t CO_2." (A middle-class American emits twenty-two tons a year.)[32] Amusingly, Gates recently published a book on climate change that gives no space to actual tax-funded climate policy (since that could potentially somewhat decrease his incredible wealth), and instead encourages middle-class people to buy expensive electric cars while hoping for new alternative jet fuels.[33]

The unflattering profile of frequent private jet flight, especially for short distances, is famously the purpose of @ElonJet, the automated social media account using flight data to post trips taken by the private jet of prominent tech entrepreneur and useless media tyrant Elon Musk. After his bizarre efforts to buy Twitter led to his legal compulsion to consummate the purchase, among his numerous ill-considered staff-shedding decisions was to ban @ ElonJet and numerous other similar accounts, then reinstate them, then require them to post on a twenty-four-hour delay.[34] Despite Musk often boasting of his commitment to free speech on his struggling platform, the account now only posts as "ElonJet but Delayed," using the handle @ElonJetNextDay. Elon's recent flights, as I look, are mostly about a half hour, few more than three hours.

While the US is correctly seen to dominate the world of private jets (or "business aviation," as the sector misleadingly prefers to call itself), the industry has grown fast in Europe. Recent research has shown that far from being used mainly to facilitate business, private aircraft are overwhelmingly used for private travel and for surprisingly short distances. A report by the European zero-emissions group Transport & Environment reached some damning conclusions, including that "close to 50% of all intra-EU private flights cover distances of less than 500 km ... These distances correspond to the operational range where planes are the least efficient," due to the higher emissions at takeoff and landing relative to cruising.[35] Observing that even conventional commercial aviation is a privilege enjoyed mostly in the developed world, flying private involves a totally different wealth level, with even "relatively affordable" jet card memberships starting at about $5,000 an hour.

More offensively, the Transport & Environment report estimates that 41 percent of private flights are empty legs, flown to move the plane to where it is needed by a wealthy owner. Of occupied flights, the average occupancy was 4.7 passengers, but regardless of passenger load "private jets are on average 10 times more carbon intensive that commercial flights." Comparison of these numbers, including quality ground transit options like European trains, is unbelievable as well:

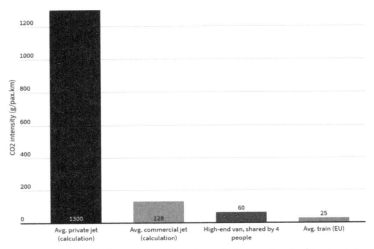

Figure 3. Comparison of CO_2 intensity of private jets and other travel modes (direct emissions only). "Private Jets: Can the Super-Rich Supercharge Zero-Emission Aviation?", *Transport & Environment*, May 2021.

The report also notes that European private "flights are mainly concentrated along the UK-France-Switzerland-Italy axis," and that the French coastal resort Nice is heavily represented among flight destinations, which "confirms that private jets are being used by wealthy people to enjoy the sun." Further, the fact that commercial flights are almost always available for the same routes leads the report to conclude that private aviation is heavily used not for business efficiency but "for rich people to get more quickly to their second homes and holiday destination." A popular French Twitter account tracks the private flights of various French billionaires, including, for example, one day in 2022 when media kingpin Vincent Bolloré made three flights between France and Greece, releasing twenty-two tons of carbon dioxide, about ten years' worth of car emissions for the average Frenchman.[36]

The French case is itself instructive. The rise of the *gilets jaunes*, or yellow vest movement, was a fascinating development that throws great light on the subject. French president Emmanuel Macron, similar perhaps to the Democratic Party's national leadership in the US, is a textbook neoliberal—socially progressive but economically conservative, relatively tolerant of growing racial and gender diversity, but "fiscally responsible" on cutting corporate taxes and limiting regulations of the corporate world. Much like the rest of liberal global leadership, Macron was eager to mollify the mounting environmental movement amid dire warnings from scientists, and so his administration imposed a tax on gasoline and diesel in an attempt to nudge French motorists to more fuel-efficient vehicles or transit options.

A popular reaction against the climate policy quickly arose that was broad and real, with large numbers of France's proud citizens participating, and for an impressively long period. Writer Vanessa Bee thoughtfully observed in *Current Affairs* that "the protesters' demands . . . are surprisingly progressive with the exception of a couple of potentially reactionary points," including a halt to the regressive fuel tax but other economically progressive pro-climate moves, like hydrogen car subsidies, raises on other fuel taxes, lower individual taxes, and an end to privatization of gas and electric utilities. Bee concludes, "The left's prints are all over this."[37]

That's because of the crucial missing chapter of the story, which is that in the previous year, Macron's neoliberal government abolished the long-standing wealth tax, or the "solidarity tax on wealth" implemented by the Socialist government in 1981. "France's Rich Get Much Richer After Abolition of Wealth Tax" was the *Forbes* headline.[38] The total effect was to reduce taxes on the wealthy and raise them on the middle and working class, which was offensive to the French regardless of the hike's potential for decreasing fossil fuel use. The World Inequality Database addressed the episode, noting the carbon tax had no "compensatory measures for low- and middle-income households. The reform was introduced at the same time as a suppression of the progressive wealth tax on financial assets and capital incomes . . . essentially concentrated among the top 1–2% of the population." On the other hand, "in British Columbia (Canada), a carbon tax was

implemented along with a significant package of transfers to low-
and middle-income households, which ensured the social viability
of the reform."[39]

But the demonstrations themselves were frequently used
by right-wing media to imply that the population was rising up
against climate taxes, rather than Macron's neoliberal redistribution of wealth upward. The conservative *Wall Street Journal* predictably claimed the "popular rage" was due to "the demonization
by political activists" of carbon dioxide, and that "voters don't
see climate change as a threat demanding personal sacrifices."[40]
Knowing French history, it's more likely that the French public,
like those around the world, has majorities in favor of climate action, but aren't willing to foot the bill themselves while the rich,
who are hugely disproportionately to blame for the problem, get
their taxes slashed. Thus, the progressive character of the yellow
vests' demands.

This episode is probably suggestive of how future neoliberal
governments will attempt to deal with climate disaster, imposing
the costs on the majority while actively continuing to exempt rich
households and their corporate property from paying any of them.
The European Union, for example, has a climate law that caps total
emissions and makes emitting firms pay based on their carbon use.
Private jets, however, are exempt from the law. Worse, France itself
enacted a climate law in 2021 barring domestic flight routes that
can be completed by train in two-and-a-half hours or less, but this
climate law applies to commercial flights, not private jet travel.[41]
So the Right's portrayal of the yellow vests as a popular uprising
against Big Government's climate laws is *connerie*.

Perhaps most damning of all, the phenomenal climate reporter Dharna Noor observed that during the 2021 Glasgow climate conference of world leaders, so many senior politicians and
business leaders were expected to fly private that the official del-
egate guide listed private airports among the conference arrival
points. Noor observed that a rock-bottom measure would be to

bar private jet travel to the world's most prominent climate conference, but that they should indeed be banned permanently.[42] Noor suggested a "soft ban" by imposing a 100 percent tax on personal jets and their cost of travel, with proceeds donated to the woefully underfunded Green Climate Fund, intended to finance poor countries' climate transition. Much of what passes for progress in climate talks is "commitments" from governments for binding emissions cuts, often not met or met years late, and difficult to take seriously when leadership can't take even the relatively painless symbolic move of avoiding private flights to climate conferences.

Private jets mean public regrets, but there is one more area where the world's plutocrats are running truly wild with their emissions. The Transport & Environment report claims that private aviation "is, without peers, the most carbon intensive activity that anyone can engage in." But unfortunately, there is one exception.

Space Waste

As noted at the front of the book, today's wealth concentration is so utterly out of hand that three billionaires have their own space programs. Hyper-billionaire, Amazon.com founder Jeff Bezos and Virgin Atlantic plutocrat Richard Branson both launched suborbital tourism flights in the summer of 2021, with Bezos's Blue Origin flights costing around $100 million. The national press are private property themselves (Bezos owns the *Washington Post*, for example), and so have gushed at the heavily choreographed launch events: "The Amazonification of space has begun in earnest. What was once largely the domain of big government is now increasingly the realm of Big Tech ... For decades, NASA did not get enough funding to do anything as epic as the Apollo program ... In contrast to the Apollo project in the 1960s, the next trip to the moon will be outsourced."[43] Of course, these jumped-up pet projects funded with laundered public dollars, and tech monopoly profits are mostly for tourism, taking billionaire geriatrics up to the edge of the atmosphere and pretending it's Star Trek.

The article quoted above actually notes that the evolution of space travel, from a costly but real government success story to private property owned by the rich, is similar to the story of the Internet.[44] Much as that technology was privatized and then talked about as if billionaire CEOs had invented it, space travel may have a similar future.

But of all the extensive talk and hype about private space travel and climate, there is frankly no better account of the new industry's climate realities than the WID's, which must be quoted at devastating length:

> Perhaps the most conspicuous illustration of extreme pollution associated with wealth inequality in recent years is the development of space travel. Space travel is expected to cost from several thousand dollars to several million dollars per trip. An 11-minute flight emits no fewer than 75 tonnes of carbon per passenger once indirect emissions are taken into account (and more likely, in the 250–1,000 tonnes range). At the other end of the distribution, about one billion individuals emit less than one tonne per person per year. Over their lifetime, this group of one billion individuals does not emit more than 75 tonnes of carbon per person. It therefore takes a few minutes in space travel to emit at least as much carbon as an individual from the bottom billion will emit in her entire lifetime. This example shows that there is scarcely any limit to the carbon emissions of the ultra-wealthy.[45]

Looking over all this, it's hard not to become really furious at people with far more money than they can ever need, who not only keep it from a world majority who desperately need resources, but are also actively destroying the future in order to yet further enrich themselves. The broad realms of business and politics are obsessively bent on this demonic, suicidal course.

People, and the planet, deserve life. The ruling class deserves extinction.

CHAPTER 6

THE CLANS

A GLOBAL SAFARI FOR
RULING-CLASS SPECIES WORLDWIDE

Let me issue and control a nation's money
and I care not who writes the laws.
—**Mayer Amschel Rothschild**[1]

Some measure of inequality is essential for the spirit
of envy and keeping up the Joneses that is, like
greed, a valuable spur to economic activity.
—**Boris Johnson**[2]

How does an American tech billionaire compare to a Russian mining oligarch? What distinguishes a Chinese manufacturing baron from a Saudi prince? What difference does it make if a ruling-class family comes from South African mining or Brazilian agribusiness? How does a Japanese *zaibatsu* compare to a Korean *chaebol*?

Every country on God's earth, rich or poor, has its own tiny awful ruling class. Regional history and local details make enormous differences, but these upper elites will reliably own whatever there is of value to own in that country and expect endless credit for telling their working classes what to do. This chapter will compare the distinct upper crusts to be found on the planet. The richness of world history and the broad diversity of elite populations worldwide means this will necessarily be a brisk survey, exploring too the most important industries for billionaire generation, conspicuously Wall Street and Silicon Valley.

In the twenty-first century few lands have been spared the rule of gold. Through relatively good times of growth or global recession, all humanity now has the same class in charge, making this a basic part of the human condition. No plane ticket will let you escape from that.

Banks for Nothing

Capitalism is famous for its long-term growth, increasing the amount of goods and services produced each year, therefore creating the possibility for a higher standard of living (depending on who gets to reap the rewards of this growth). For firms to grow and build a new factory or food processing plant or cell phone tower, they need money—liquid capital that can be spent, or invested, to build up production. Even cash-rich companies like Apple and Exxon don't cover most of their expansion through cash on hand—they finance it. They get bank loans or mortgages, or issue bonds, but in all cases the key to growth is access to capital.

Banks, or the financial services industry if you prefer, are the private institutions that collect this capital from depositors and can bundle it into loans to businesses (or people, as with mortgages). This puts bankers in the most influential position in the economy—everyone big and small must come to them for capital, and they tend to become uniquely knowledgeable about what's happening in the market economy. Thus, banks often emerge as the most powerful companies, and bankers the most powerful figures, within capitalism.

This has had some mighty dramatic manifestations, as in the example mentioned earlier of J. P. Morgan bailing out the US Treasury twice in one year (see chapter 3). As it was in Morgan's time, today banks are at the heart of capitalism's drive for company growth and market dominance. Morgan's Wall Street trust utterly dominated finance at the turn of the last century, when America came to have the world's biggest economy. But then came the New Deal with its regulations cutting back on monopolies and putting limits even on the oligopolies. Banking in particular was targeted, as it was seen to be too powerful, not to mention that it was widely considered responsible for the Black Tuesday crash that kicked off the decade-long Great Depression.

So, the banks were broken up along state lines, prohibiting them from merging with or buying banks in other states; and along industry lines, so the main street commercial banks holding regular peoples' deposits couldn't go into investment banking, the risky world of high finance on Wall Street. Almost as if these limitations were successful, the New Deal era saw no major financial crises. But once the Reagan Revolution brought neoliberal deregulation to the industry, that changed fast. Companies went on a giant merger binge in the 1990s and 2000s, creating today's "megabanks." It was these colossal banks—JPMorgan Chase, Bank of America, Wells Fargo, and Citigroup—that made the bad bets on subprime mortgages in the 2000s that led to the enormous finance crash of 2008.[3]

Banks today are regulated, but largely on their own terms since the Obama administration left the reregulation job to Congress where the banks have deep influence, and megabanks today remain gigantic and powerful. When bank runs broke out on a number of midsize lenders like Silicon Valley Bank and First Republic in 2023, the government again acted aggressively to insure all deposits (even those above the FDIC cap) and avoid large depositor losses. Our weary world has definitely not seen its last panicky finance crash, but the industry's top figures remain just about the most senior members of the world's ruling class. They also remain notorious in the business world and media depictions as gigantic, awful, bullying, coke-blasting economy-ruiners.

And so it was from their ranks that Jeffrey Epstein emerged, a millionaire financier with ties to major billionaires like Leslie Wexner, who had a long career as a pretender and a predator. Epstein courted the really rich as clients, cultivated Ivy League academics, and passed strangely through circles of elite power. Epstein is also infamous, of course, for his monstrous record as a serial sex offender, who somehow managed to receive a lenient sentence on the charges from his first conviction for solicitation of a minor for prostitution.

This didn't stop him from endeavoring to turn his modest fortune into elevated contacts with elite power brokers by, among other things, flying to his private island with men from the highest circles. Men like former US president Bill Clinton, celebrity attorney Alan Dershowitz, former Microsoft CEO Bill Gates, and Prince Andrew of the UK were all flown to Epstein's private island, where testimony has since revealed Epstein kept young women in conditions of nightmarish sexual subjugation.[4] None of these men have so far been legally proven to have engaged in underage sex on Epstein's trips, with the partial exception of Andrew, who settled a court case and has seen his role in the royal family diminished. On the other hand, the record is clear that none of these men have scruples against ruining the lives of thousands of people in industries where they oversaw or enabled decades of brutal outsourcing, or reckless mangling of the social safety net. Thus, flying on a private jet to a private island and partaking in the exploitation of fetching runaways doesn't really seem beneath them.

Epstein of course was later indicted, only to die in prison under somewhat suspicious circumstances, leading to speculation that he may have had blackmail information on his powerful guests. He did indeed appear to blackmail Gates, using his knowledge of a separate affair of Gates's to demand he contribute money to a charitable fund Epstein was setting up.[5]

Today, as this book has reviewed, bankers struggle to understand why they're so unpopular. But they absolutely pioneered the reborn Gilded Age elite lifestyle in the modern world, with stratospheric pay, crush-my-rivals ruthlessness, weird shiny Wall Street suits, and perks from corner offices to putting the cocaine inhaled off a sex worker's ass on the company credit card. Wall Street set the tone for the modern capitalist owning class, and what do you know—it turns out they're evil assholes.

Forbes magazine noted in 2023 that the finance and technology industries lead the way in creating the "ultra-rich," along with classic standbys like manufacturing and retail.[6] Having covered banking, let's turn now to the hyped-up world of the tech industry.

Siliconned

For some years, Americans were in love with Big Tech. The Internet, online video, then mobile apps, and streaming—so much fun! Everyone went whole hog and put all their information onto online platforms and signed terabyte-length terms of service agreements without reading them. But after a few blissful years, it became apparent these companies couldn't be bothered to spend money protecting all that private data, were steering people into conspiracy theory rabbit holes to maximize interactions, and were tracking your every move.

Only then did America wake up to how colossal and powerful the giant platform companies have become, but by that point it was too late. As I wrote in *Bit Tyrants: The Political Economy of Silicon Valley*, tech platforms are powered by "network effects"—the ability of communication-based services to gain value as more people use them. The first user of a telephone or online video hub has little to do; it's only when others start using them that they actually get useful. And the more users a service has, the more content creators it attracts, and thus more users. This network effect creates an unusually strong tendency toward monopoly—incumbent firms tend to attract new users, and soon the advantage is "locked in." Even the hyper-capitalist *Economist* magazine called the online platforms "straight out of the box" monopolies.[7]

Relatively early on in the dominant platforms' digestion of the industry, the conservative *Wall Street Journal* ran a cover article with a flying saucer with corporate logos beaming users aboard, under the headline "Facebook, Amazon and Other Tech Giants Tighten Grip on Internet Economy." It described plainly that "the Internet economy is powered by an infrastructure . . . controlled by a small handful of tech giants," naming Microsoft, Apple, Amazon, Facebook, and Google as "established companies [that] dominate in essential services that both fuel and extract value from the rising digital economy . . . Anyone starting a business needs to make sure they can be found on Google. Anyone with goods to sell wants Amazon to carry them."[8]

By now several of the tech platforms are trillion-dollar corporations, and their leaders have become the newest nouveau riche to ascend to capitalism's ruling class. Their dumb dressed-down look, their imbecilic repetition of "disruption" and "Uber-of-this" lingo, and their striving for monopoly have reshaped the style and conversation of ruling elites around the world.

Big Tech is thoroughly bound up in everything we do, from working to exercising to dating to watching TV. The industry has proved politically powerful enough to stop all efforts in the US to regulate it, although the Europeans have had more success, instituting bloc-wide rules (that often become globally observed by the platforms) requiring local storage of data, limits to tracking software, the right of users to control their data, and more.

But tech isn't going anywhere, and indeed has now become arguably codominant with Wall Street as the central sector of modern capitalism. Whatever the future of humanity is, Silicon Valley is tightly bound up with it, and there's no delete key in the world that can remove their incredible power and all-seeing eyes.

Engulfed

Past these key industries, we can explore the broader world of the ruling class. The rulers of today's Arab states around the Persian Gulf mostly owe the survival of their monarchies to Britain and America. Britain cultivated the local Gulf elites in the nineteenth century, and the modern Kingdom of Saudi Arabia only arose between the World Wars, with American blessing as the House of Saud took control of the realm and the most holy Islamic sites. The region has one of the world's most unequal wealth landscapes, with its richest 1 percent of households owning a stupendous 44 percent of the regional wealth.[9] Royalty of the Gulf states are famous for their stratospheric oil fortunes—one prince was reported to have lost $6 million in a single night at Monte Carlo.[10]

The regimes of these countries are also some of the ugliest, most nakedly authoritarian ruling classes in the world. The royal families have spent their decades in power locking up opponents, closing independent media, repressing their Shiite minorities, and buying off their subjects with slices of the thundering river of oil money that made these hideous regimes the best friends of the West. No elections, women often must be covered head to toe and cannot go out without a male escort, just literal gross feudal monarchy. Yet every postwar American president has staged photo ops with these kings and princes as they sought to maintain control over global energy supplies, a move that pretty drastically undermines the regular claims of Western governments that they respect freedom and human rights.

The Arab monarchies, and especially the Gulf states, are also highly reliant on hyper-exploited migrant labor, mostly from South Asia. In small, arid states with low populations that wish to use oil wealth for upward mobility, there are limited options for a blue-collar workforce to build the insane new buildings, wait on wealthy subjects, or care for the children of the Gulf's middle classes. The Gulf states are so reliant on foreign labor that migrant workers came to represent "the majority of the population within most Gulf states," as the best book on the subject puts it, kept un-der control by having "their political and economic rights . . . care-fully restricted and managed. The possibility to obtain property, form unions and own capital were outlawed."[11]

This reliance on borderline slave labor only reached real Western public awareness in 2022 when the World Cup was set in Qatar, a petrostate thought to have high standards of living for their local subjects. During the Games, journalists were oc-casionally allowed into notoriously private Qatari homes. Ac-counts describe large estates with multiple guesthouses, tended by groundskeepers from East Africa and South Asia. A wealthy Qatari suggests, "The minute you say, 'salaam alaikum'—'hello,' you know—you give them a lot. They just feel respected." The au-thor of the piece goes on to describe a gender-segregated female group of affluent Qataris watching a game, during which "every few minutes, staff members wearing purple dresses and white cotton gloves made the rounds with trays brimming with bowls of sweets, cappuccinos in gold-rimmed cups and a pot of Arabic coffee. One passed by with a bouquet of flowers so large that I could see only the legs of the housekeeper carrying it." All this in a "highly stratified" country, with "approximately two million mi-grant laborers enlisted to facilitate a luxurious lifestyle for about 380,000 Qatari citizens."[12]

In Dubai, laborers from the Indian subcontinent are re-cruited and go into debt for their flights to the Gulf, and have their passports seized on arrival, making them utterly helpless to their overseers "in modern-day bondage, and [have] no choice but to continue to work in the searing heat in order to pay back their debts." Foreigners (semi-slaves and rich expats) are 80 percent of the population.[13]

Today, the monarchs are eager for tourism and foreign in-vestment, and are looking to clean up their reputations. For Saudi Arabia, by far the largest, most influential, and most economically important Gulf state, the stakes are higher. The current wretched godforsaken monarch to rule that accursed land, Crown Prince Mohammed bin Salman, is campaigning to lessen the kingdom's reliance on oil and gas exports. To do so, he began by wringing wealth out of his own awful royal family, once by keeping fellow princes and other family members against their will for weeks at the Riyadh Ritz-Carlton until they coughed up a few million for the cause.

To come up with cash, Saudi princes sold off incredible assets, including $600 million in art, real estate, and yachts. This included "a $155 million British country estate, two yachts more than 200 feet long, and Mughal jewels gifted as wedding presents by a late king." Some royals "with large staffs and lavish lifestyles" were spending upwards of $30 million a month. Now bin Salman is charging a tax on them: $2,500 a year "for each domestic worker beyond the fourth employee, costing some royals hundreds of thousands of dollars a year."[14]

Much of the extorted money goes into the Prince Salman's utterly daffy ideas, such as Neom, a desert city meant to be a futuristic "smart city" where all services run on personal technology, part of The Line, a fever dream of a development planned to run a mile long and just 660 feet wide, standing 1,600 feet tall with mirrored walls.[15] Projected to cost several hundred billion dollars, the alleged city would be monitored by AI using predictive data models to improve city life. This fully stupid quick-fix development fantasy is the kind of thing you get with deluded child monarchs surrounded by ball-fondling sycophants, and probably not the very best use of an incomprehensible amount of money in a country with plenty of desperately poor people.

Another part of the royal family's cash is going to clean up the kingdom's image, tainted by little petty offenses such as never holding elections, keeping women in conditions associated with the Taliban, suppressing the Shiite minority, and lopping off the heads of criminals. One way of cleaning up reputations, also used by Russian oligarchs (see below), is buying up popular British football teams. The Saudis bought longtime underdog UK football team Newcastle United shortly after Manchester City was also bought by Abu Dhabi via intermediaries. In response to this naked attempt to improve the image of an ugly medieval dictatorship, fans cheered and gathered "in thobes and headdresses, waving the Saudi flag, inscribed with the shahada, while singing that their club had, at last, been returned to them."[16]

And yet it's easy come, easy go, because countries run by autocrats often have a hard time sticking with a plan. With billions in play to change the kingdom's reputation, in 2018 the crown prince learned that a critical Saudi journalist, Jamal Khashoggi, had entered the Saudi consulate in Istanbul to get documents for his coming marriage. Khashoggi never left the consulate. The Saudis have changed their story about what happened; however, the Turks and the CIA have reached the same conclusion: the prince had Khashoggi killed in the embassy, dismembered his body, and smuggled it out in duffel bags.[17]

Later, a ruling-class friendship between the crown prince and Amazon founder and billionaire Jeff Bezos fell apart. The two had been in touch for some time about Amazon building a data center in the kingdom with the typical enormous government subsidies. And when this deal fell through, pictures were leaked from Bezos's phone showing racy images of his mistress. The Saudis denied involvement, and it turned out to have apparently been Bezos's mistress's brother who leaked the pictures, but the friendship was over—the Wall Street Journal calls the two "archenemies."[18]

The Gulf monarchs look set to continue trying to balance their own absolute autocratic medieval power with enough modernization to attract foreign capital and friendly media puff pieces. But there aren't enough duffel bags in the world to carry out the dismembered body of Arab freedom.

LOLigarchs

And it was all going so well.

Prior to Russian president Vladimir Putin's ill-fated decision to invade Ukraine in 2022, the Russian rich had largely succeeded in joining their Western and global counterparts as members of the world's owning class. Their purchases of priceless art were cleared, their kids enrolled in elite Western academies, and their yachts docked next to craft owned by their American, European, and Chinese peers. Even Putin's original 2014 invasion of Ukraine, which brought sanctions on the country and the early rumblings of the renewed Cold War with Russia, still left Russia's oligarchs integrated into the global ruling class.

The oligarchs themselves only arose with the collapse of the Soviet Union in 1991. Under the "shock therapy" approach insisted on by US consultants, the Soviet economy was sold off to anyone who could come up with the widely distributed vouchers, through honest or crooked methods. Within a few years, the legacy of Soviet industrialization was in the hands of a tiny number of hyper-rich, super-evil Russian capitalists often called "oligarchs," from a classic Greek term for rich rulers. The rule of the oligarchs in the 1990s was so ugly and brazen that when Putin first came to power in 2000, originally with their support, his mandate was to bring them back under control. At that time, the World Bank estimated that the thirty richest oligarchs controlled an unbelievable 40 percent of Russian GDP.[19]

Under this entente, the oligarchs didn't interfere with politics or complain too much when Putin's state locked up political opponents—a perennial activity in Russia—or nationalized certain strategic sectors, especially energy. And the state didn't stand in the way of their riches, which the oligarchs heaped up with stunning abandon. To this day, the region is one of the most unequal on earth, with a whopping 46 percent of its capital held by the richest 1 percent.[20]

Kampfner recounts how the oligarchs turned London's high-end real estate market into "Londongrad":

Former British government ministers queued up to represent them in the House of Lords. Spin-doctors did their PR, tasking juniors in the office to "improve" their clients' Wikipedia entries—the internet made it easier to launder reputations, but also easier to be found out . . . Several law firms helped Russians to use Britain's hideously indulgent defamation culture to slap suits on enquiring journalists at the first sign of trouble.[21]

By far the most common form of oligarchic conspicuous consumption has been yachts. Selling one to an oligarch "all starts with NDAs," for the broker, the shipbuilders, and the crew. Russian yacht owners, like American and European ones, have tastes that can run the final bill for a luxury boat up to the hundreds of millions of dollars. The *Times* breaks it down: $28 million for the steel hull, $24 million for the fancy deck, $21 million for the engine room, and $18 million just for paint. There are crazy add-ons too, like $2 million for a movie theater or $2 to $3 million for fully ventilated Kevlar-lined safe rooms. "Some billionaires even build their own medical units, complete with nurses and doctors."[22] Upkeep is usually about 10 percent of the yacht's build price, plus docking fees for a giant boat that can run $29,000 a week, or $750,000 annually.

Since the start of the Russo-Ukrainian War, only some nations' ports, like Turkey and the UAE, remain open to the cruising oligarch. With Russia sanctioned over its war crimes in Ukraine, just flying their private jets has become almost impossible. Dozens of them are now sitting on the tarmac at Dubai's Al Maktoum International Airport, at a cost of about $1,000 a day. Dubai allows them in, but because the planes can mostly no longer be insured or serviced due to sanctions, they are largely stuck there.[23]

Getting Western goods is also difficult, no small concern for buyers working for ultrarich oligarch households. Cars, smartphones, and clothes are still entering Russia to satisfy oligarch demand, mostly through friendlier third countries like Turkey and Kazakhstan. A Dubai luxury car showroom director of communications said, "The wealthy people always stay wealthy," finding the war "did not affect them."[24] Many rich Russians have moved temporarily to Turkey, which has not joined the Western sanctions regime. The press notes that "newly arrived Russians are buying as many as four apartments at a time, usually with cash, in order to invest the $250,000 required for citizenship" (see chapter 2).[25]

Meanwhile, as the horror of war grinds on in Ukraine and refugees continue to flee the fighting, bombing, and threats, it's fair to note that once again the rich fled first. The *Financial Times* has covered how "from private schools to cosmetic surgery clinics, restaurants and upmarket estate agents, Polish businesses catering to the well-heeled are adapting to a new influx of customers: wealthy Ukrainians fleeing Russia's war. While a majority of refugees were forced to escape their country with few possessions, a smaller group of relatively affluent Ukrainians arrived in their own cars and have provided an unexpected boost to upmarket businesses amid an economic slowdown." Private schools, cosmetic surgery clinics, and high-end shopping are benefiting from the exodus of Ukrainian oligarchs.[26]

When Russia's rich can rejoin their brothers and sisters in the world's ruling class is unclear. At the time of writing this book, the Russo-Ukrainian War grinds on, looking at the moment increasingly like a war of attrition or full-on stalemate. When this eventuates in talks and eventual peace is obviously unknowable, and until then the war will have many victims—dead civilians, displaced refugee families, rising hunger in the developing world from lack of Russian and Ukrainian food exports, and the destroyed environment of east Ukraine, littered with unexploded cluster bombs and poisonous depleted uranium rounds.

But there will be one more victim—the sad oligarchs who can only yacht to Turkey or the UAE due to sanctions, and whose

Western imports are more expensive due to extra middlemen. The Russian tragedy carries on.

Great Cabal of China

China, for all its surviving Maoist iconography and its definitely still-ruling Communist Party, is a classic capitalist state today. Starting with special economic zones, China began opening up its economy to foreign investment in the late 1980s, which American and European corporations were delighted to provide. They invested to create a cheap export platform for products formerly made domestically with expensive first-world workers, and of course also for access to China's own enormous domestic market.

There's a great deal of Western animosity now toward China, but it's somewhat strange since China did what we wanted—open up the economy. China, however, also did what the West did, which was to retain a strong enough state to guide actual economic development that benefited the country, rather than what the Third World was forced to do (see below). For decades the Chinese government would hold large summits and meetings with executives of Western corporate CEOs, with senior political leadership meeting heads of Blackstone, AIG, Carlyle, BP, Pepsi, Walmart, and Coca-Cola, just looking at one 2013 meeting.[27]

Having a tyrannical state is far from anti-capitalist—the sadly most common mode of economic development is authoritarian, from the Gilded Age autocrats to Stalin to postwar Japan to today's China. Most developing-world countries have tyrannical governments and market economies, but China's government has managed something few other developing-world countries have— they have used the things the West insists will bring development, like foreign direct investment, in a way that *actually did* develop the country. China now has many capitalist features, including a rich owning class—the country's richest 1 percent owns 30.5 percent of its wealth, one of the relatively lower shares globally.[28]

Other economists, including the great inequality scholar Branko Milanovic, express some hope that Chinese inequality may fall thanks to classic mitigating factors like widening access to education and potentially more social welfare, suggesting "one can be optimistic that China's income inequality may have peaked." Yet, he also notes the countercurrents of corruption and fast-rising wealth that tend to increase the share of national income going to capital, which is always highly concentrated.[29] China's long-running troubles with its large housing-construction companies and measly social safety net mitigate against these hopeful possibilities.

Either way, as is common around the capitalist world, China's rich can defend themselves. A *New York Times* headline ran, "Billionaire Lawmakers Ensure the Rich Are Represented in China's Legislature," finding "among the 1,271 richest Chinese people tracked by the Shanghai-based Hurun Report, a record 203, or more than one in seven, are delegates to the nation's Parliament or its advisory body."[30] Kampfner observes the National People's Congress is

> by far the wealthiest legislature of any country . . . [I]ts seventy richest members make more than the total net worth of all members of all three branches of the US state . . . From the days of the Tang and Ming dynasties, China's elite has been careful to hide its wealth behind high walls. Sales of luxury items are rampant among the top 1 per cent, but where possible the acquisitions—or the identities of the purchasers—are kept out of sight. Limousines invariably come with blacked-out windows; fine wines are drunk in restaurants hidden away in secure compounds. In November 2013, the world's most expensive case of wine—a 1978 Burgundy, Romanée-Conti—sold at Christie's in Hong Kong for $476,000, to a Chinese bidder.[31]

Modern China is more capitalist, in fact, than many realize. A drive by President Xi Jinping to reduce inequality with a "common prosperity" plan was meant to address "concerns that elites had benefited disproportionately from the country's economic boom," the *Wall Street Journal* reports. But Beijing "walked back some measures," including "plans to expand a new property tax that could have funded social-welfare programs, but faced opposition from elites and policy makes [*sic*] who worried it would push property values lower." Notably, "China's tax system is less progressive than developed countries', with burdens falling mostly on lower-income workers. Raising tax rates on the upper class, who tend to be more politically connected, has faced resistance . . . Personal income taxes in China add up to 1.2% of gross domestic product, compared with about 10% in the U.S. and U.K."[32] Experts suggest the government "introduce inheritance or capital-gains taxes on individuals, which would redirect more wealth from richer families, but that would also likely face opposition." The major analogues are countries with great historic rivalries with China, above all Japan and Korea, which both relied heavily on state guidance and subsidies to build up their postwar electronics and automotive sectors, rather than a market-based approach that would have seen them carry on with their existing comparative advantage in rice and fish. All these economies used state-based development models, mostly under authoritarian conditions—the US occupation authority in Japan, and the US-backed Park dictatorship in South Korea—and all succeeded by breaking Western rules.

The Chinese ruling class of businessmen, tech leaders, and government functionaries is as self-interested and cruel as any other, but it is one of the few that is not actively desiring another major global conflict, one we would be unlikely to survive with our civilization intact. Here's hoping the Middle Kingdom takes the high road.

Old Colonials

Europe's ruling class has had a hell of a ride, fully dominating the world for a couple hundred years. Covering the world's map in the colors of its western states, European colonialism gave a majority of the planet's countries a shared origin story: having a war to drive out some European imperialists.

Wealth in the western European countries rose sharply with the Industrial Revolution, when traditional social and natural systems were digested as industrial inputs for early capitalism. Industrialization kept Europe in charge of its colonies until the world wars, which first weakened and then broke their hold over Africa and Asia, with Latin America having kicked out its Iberian colonists earlier only to become economic satellites of Britain and then America.

After World War II, the Europeans lost their empires, despite Churchill's best efforts to maintain British control of the great prize of India. Since then, labor and social democratic movements led postwar Europe to develop a system of social supports that is the envy of the rest of the world. Despite waves of austerity in the neoliberal period, much of these national health-care and educational systems have persisted.

But since the wars, the European ruling class has been completely subordinated to the direction of America. Incorporation into the NATO military alliance has played a major role in this, including its gradual expansion to the east despite regular Russian insistence that this is unacceptable. After NATO looked weakened by the erratic and isolationist aspects of the Trump administration, it came surging back after the outbreak of the Russo-Ukrainian War. European acquiescence to American foreign policy and even economic decisions has gone on, like expelling Chinese Huawei technology and cutting off the country's access to cutting-edge semiconductor printers manufactured in the Netherlands.

As mentioned previously, Europe has the least crazily lopsided wealth distribution today, with the richest 1 percent of households owning a mere 25 percent of the region's capital.[33] Still, it's a more inheritance-based ruling elite than in America, and the older rich families, frequently ones with royal or noble backgrounds, or at least historic connections to state power, are some of the most insufferably arrogant and literally entitled in the world. Rich families expect respect and are very accustomed to being able to tell schoolmates that they can buy their families, giving the European Old Money rich the exact characteristics that aristocrats are mocked for worldwide.

The richest man in Europe, Bernard Arnault, and his family have already been mentioned in this book. Arnault is presently auditioning his adult children to run various arms of the luxury goods conglomerate the family controls and which makes Arnault intermittently the richest man on Earth. The kids hold seats on the board of the holding company that gives the family control of the company and are expected to inherit various senior positions in it over time.[34]

Germany, as Europe's most dynamic economy, is far from exempt. A subject of some national reflection is the continued prominence of the classic German industrial families, many dirtied with crimes against humanity during World War II but still national economic champions today. The definitive text on this particular sector of the European ruling class is David de Jong's irresistible *Nazi Billionaires*. It artfully describes the long relationship between the powerful country's rich industrial families, beginning with support for the democracy-hating, free-market-loving early Nazi Party, and culminating in running grossly enlarged wartime industries with thousands of enslaved POWs and Jews.

Today, some younger members of these families would prefer we all move on from the past. Verena Bahlsen, 26-year-old inheritor of the great Bahlsen confectionery company, scolded a socialist politician who advocated for the common ownership of Germany's biggest industrial companies by saying: "I am a capitalist . . . I own a quarter of Bahlsen and I am happy about it, too. It should continue to belong to me. I want to make money and buy sailing yachts from my dividend and stuff."[35]

But the ultimate example of this inherited wealth is, of course, the various European royal families, above all the House of Windsor in the UK, which is technically one of the richest in the world, although much of their assets are fixed by hoary royal institutions and customs. Thus, although they throw off quite large streams of income, they broadly can't be disposed of like other forms of wealth. King George VI famously referred to the family and its interests as "The Firm," and its assets include a large real estate portfolio in the Crown Estate, including choice assets in London, plus the Duchies of Cornwall and Lancaster, which together are worth over £16 billion, according to the *Financial Times*.[36] Plus you got your various palaces, racehorses, and gigantic precious stones with dumb names like the Koh-i-Noor diamond.

Still, Danny Dorling notes in his book *Inequality and the 1%* that the estimated wealth of the whole UK 1 percent is about £110 billion: "For the price of the richest 1 per cent in Britain, we could instead support 1,100 royal families ... and the superrich don't even smile and wave."[37]

There's no Old Money like Old World Old Money.

Third World, Last Place

Everyone knows that there are many extremely poor countries in the world, sometimes called the Third World, or these days the "developing world." These countries are often seen as scary, struggling places, with billions of people trapped in grinding poverty across the poor regions of Africa, southern Asia, and Latin America.

But these countries have been The Poor Countries for quite some time now. At the end of World War II, the great states of the developing world, like Brazil, Indonesia, India, and the Congo, were dramatically poorer than the developed world. Today, seventy-five years later, they're still poor. Just what the hell is going on here?

For centuries, most of today's developing world was part of the colonial systems of the European powers, including Britain's hold on India and Egypt, French ownership of West Africa and Vietnam, the Netherlands' possession of Indonesia, the Belgian Congo, Portuguese Brazil, and so on. Colonies were used as sources of vital materials, from precious Eastern spices used to rescue bland European cooking, to desperately needed oil to fuel the West's industrial economy. The colonies were also often barred from importing products from other European powers, making them important "captive markets" of their mother countries. And in addition to these economic incentives, the countries' territories were treated like chess pieces in the rivalries of the great powers.

After the imperial powers were beaten, exhausted, and occupied during World War II, the developing world launched movements for independence—and the Europeans fought doggedly to avoid giving it to them. From French Algeria to British India, the colonial powers used ungodly violence and torture on a huge scale against dissidents, keeping cruel pro-Western regimes in office as long as possible. As the developing countries of the Global South gradually won independence in long, bloody struggles, their traumatized societies fell under what leftists often call "neocolonialism"—using local dictators installed and supported by the rich Western states to run these newly independent countries, thus allowing Western companies to continue owning many of the crucial resources and selling products to their large markets.

One of the most valuable tools to keep these countries from real independence has been debt. The battle-scarred governments arising from the wars of independence—with some authoritarian and some managing to remain partially republican—demanded compensation from the former imperial powers. This was in recognition of the scale of their crimes against the Third World, from the enormous violence unleashed against them to the significant part of their wealth that was stripped and invested to build up Western economies. Europe and the US refused; however, they frequently indicated they were prepared to *lend* them money instead.

Despite constant requests for capital grants as reparations rather than lines of credit, many developing countries borrowed money, ostensibly for development—investing in education, health, and domestic infrastructure to begin the journey to a developed-world standard of living. Frequently these loans were organized by the World Bank, created by the Western powers after World War II to help provide "development credit" to the Third World. These loans for roads, bridges, schools, and hospitals were supposed to be paid for by the countries' great future economic growth, although notably the World Bank and Western investors favored projects that built on the poor countries' existing comparative trade advantages. This meant exporting basic goods like bulk crops or raw commodities like oil and copper—largely leaving the higher value-added processing and manufacturing to the developed world.

But the numerous right-wing authoritarians installed by the US in the Cold War environment were extremely corrupt, including the Shah of Iran, the fascist Brazilian military government, and the string of US-backed dictators in Pakistan. The countries borrowed giant amounts from international banks in the Western countries in the name of the world's penniless, but the money went straight up their rulers' noses, while the debts stayed on the books despite being clearly "odious"—debt that should be canceled due to illegitimacy. According to the World Bank, by 2010 the "external debt" owed by poor Third World states had reached an outrageous, towering $4 trillion.[38]

And it's even more offensive when you consider where these giant sums from poor people go. Developing world debt—the bonds issued by sovereign borrowers like governments in the Global South—is held widely, but like most financial assets, public debt from the developing world is held mostly by financial institutions and wealthy investors in the developed world. The atrocity of this really needs to be considered—you have the most grindingly poor people on the godforsaken planet remitting quite large sums of cash to the richest people and institutions in the world, taking from Malala to give to Donald Trump Jr.

But the giant loans from the World Bank and private foreign investors failed to enable the needed economic growth—in part because of the inherently limited, commodity export–based development model, and also because much of the money went into corrupt dictators' Swiss bank accounts. And when inadequate growth left the countries unable to readily pay their debts, creditors called the IMF—the International Monetary Fund.

Mind the SAP

Originally created to help regulate capital flows, the IMF was constituted alongside the World Bank in the famous Bretton Woods global financial policy summit in 1944. But by the 1980s the IMF had evolved into the credit community's enforcer—developing countries that fell behind on their debt payments would find lenders wouldn't extend them further credit, except for the IMF. But the Fund has become infamous worldwide for the policy changes it requires before extending new loans, known as SAPs—structural adjustment programs. Allegedly these are meant to help countries stabilize their finances, giving lenders confidence that the countries can manage their debt and resume economic growth. However, the policies are a recipe for satisfying wealthy foreign ruling-class lenders above all else, often at the expense of recession or long-term stagnation in these painfully poor countries, through aggressive "austerity" programs.

For example, SAPs typically include fiscal austerity—fixing the government's budget deficit by cutting social spending. The main targets usually include health and education spending, as well as subsidies—spending by the state to lower prices for basic food and fuel, like cooking or heating oil. For the global poor, these subsidies are often life-and-death concerns, making the difference that keeps families from having to choose between food and keeping the heat on, and so they're often the most forcefully publicly demanded government policies. But they are a fiscal drag on the poorest states because huge numbers of desperate people rely on them, and they make an obvious target for IMF policy writers. SAPs also require new, highly regressive taxes, usually on the poor or small middle classes.

SAPs also require monetary austerity and privatization, where a public agency is sold off to private investors, such as health clinics or major infrastructure like ports. This helps the government budget but means people must pay for formerly free services, and comes with large layoffs as the newly private agencies try to make money, damn the cost. The ruling elites of these nations end up having their interests protected, whether these are large landholdings (the classic developing-world ruling-class asset) or major former public property, like ports or telecommunications systems.

The great Marxist writer Vijay Prashad uses the example of the small south African state of Malawi, which after a disastrous privatization of its agricultural development agency saw prices of basic grains shoot up 400 percent, which along with alternating floods and droughts brought full-on starvation. The IMF did not consider this adequate cause to amend the SAP, and Malawi spends more annually on its debt service than on health, education, and agriculture put together.[39]

So the IMF's SAPs, along with other Third World calamities, have kept the developing world in a perpetual state of "development" for many decades now, by turning them into debt-servicing machines. Don't take my word for it—the late archconservative economist (and archenemy of mine) Milton Friedman himself said, "IMF bailouts are hurting the countries they are lending to, and benefitting the foreigners who lent to them. The United States does give foreign aid. But this is a different kind of foreign aid. It only goes through countries like Thailand to Bankers Trust."[40] The IMF then is an important part of the global systems of control, making it a long shot for a social movement to not only gain state power anywhere in the world, but also preventing any real left-wing government from taking any steps to reform its economy. Strapped governments ordered to implement austerity can't redistribute wealth for great social programs, so along with other entities like the financial markets and the US military, the global ruling class has yet more defensive tools to stop any popular struggles for socialism or other popular political movements.

And so as decades pass, large countries containing enormous wealth, like Brazil, Indonesia, and the Congo, somehow remain grindingly poor (although their top households stay fabulously rich). This is neocolonialism—the component of neoliberalism that maintains the people of the Third World in debt traps, and which looks not all that different from classic colonialism. After so many decades of failed promises, even the IMF has been forced to recognize the real effects of its SAPs—in a truly incredible IMF paper titled "Neoliberalism: Oversold?" staff economists report, "Instead of delivering growth, some neoliberal policies have increased inequality, in turn jeopardizing durable expansion . . . Austerity policies . . . hurt demand—and thus worsen employment and unemployment . . . [E]pisodes of fiscal consolidation have been followed, on average, by drops rather than by expansions in output."[41] Yet new IMF lending programs for states like Argentina and Pakistan still have the reliable austerity-heavy terms, like previous "bailouts"—not bailouts of the countries, but bailouts of the countries' ruling-class creditors. It is a darkly hilarious fact that there's an entire category of urban and rural uprising known as "IMF riots," which reliably erupt after some proud, poor country is racked with SAP austerity.

Often IMF SAPs require explicit repudiation of political programs that won mass support. Pakistan is a clear case of this global class warfare, where Prime Minister Imran Khan ran for office on a popular program of jobs and welfare—more health and education spending, and employment to raise the quality of life for this fast-growing population. But finding the state close to defaulting on its debt, his government has been largely forced to "shred his political program," as the *Wall Street Journal* reported, and "raise tax rates, curb government spending and increase gas and electricity prices in return for IMF support."[42] Calling his country's condition a "debt trap," Khan hopes the country can return to growth after the SAP, but the bailout isn't even a sure thing since "the U.S. government, which holds sway over the IMF," is concerned that Pakistan will use the bailout funds to repay large loans to China instead. It's worth noting that, as the new program continues to weaken the economy and "stifle demand," this is Pakistan's twenty-second IMF program, all of which have been overseen by a string of successive US-backed military dictators, from Zia-ul-Haq to Pervez Musharraf.[43]

Through it all, these countries face horribly widespread hunger, malnutrition, and even famine. Years ago even the conservative *Financial Times* recognized that "there is a problem of distribution, to be sure, but it is more to do with money than with food. People are not hungry these days because food supplies are not available; they are hungry because they are poor."[44] The IMF is a major tool of today's global ruling class, as the *Financial Times* also said: "The fall of the Soviet bloc has . . . create[d] a new imperial age," with "a system of indirect rule that has involved the integration of leaders of developing countries into the network of the new ruling class."[45]

Like a family reunion you don't want to get invited to, the world's ruling class has a family resemblance that's hard to look at. For all their enormous diversity of historical backgrounds, paths to great wealth, and local peculiarities, the owning classes look a lot alike the world over. They hoard whatever wealth is to be had in the land, rule over the hapless subjects or citizens living there, and demand nonstop celebration and praise for their alleged efforts at creating jobs, public service, or defending of the faith.

But every elite's time in the sun ends someday. For the final chapter, let's look into bringing that day closer.

CHAPTER 7

THE PLAN

THE SOCIALIST MOVEMENT TO STICK IT TO THE MAN

The rights and interests of the laboring man will be protected and cared for by the Christian men to whom God has given control of the property rights of the country. Pray earnestly that right may triumph, always remembering that the Lord God Omnipotent still reigns.
—George F. Baer, president, Philadelphia and Reading Railroad[1]

[T]he low-skilled American worker is the most overpaid worker in the world.
—Hedge fund manager[2]

Today's ruling class towers over us, and commands the major economic and political institutions. They shape how economies will work through control of investment, and control the ideas people encounter through their ownership of the dominant private media. Every as-seen-on-TV argument to justify their towering power and debased waste collapses immediately when scrutinized, so they do their best to make sure that scrutiny is carefully avoided.

Beyond scrutinizing the rich, though, there are ways to deal with their control over society. Traditional social democratic measures, like heavy progressive taxes on high-income households, or tight regulation of their corporate empires, remain popular and achievable today, and we should continue pursuing them. But a more effective approach would be to "expropriate" the ruling class—to take away their large-scale property, so that they no longer own and get to control the economy. Every factory, giant farm, data center, oil refinery, and goods warehouse is owned by a rich person, family, or class, giving them their gigantic incomes and social power. Past efforts to put the rich in their box, like European social democracy or the US New Deal, mostly failed at this decisive step, leaving the rich with the cash and social influence to mount a major comeback thanks to the neoliberalism of the last forty years. If we get another chance, we should avoid making the same mistake.

But the men and women of today's ruling class are far from invincible. Our side has won victories large and small in the workplace, and in politics. Today's labor movement and the surprising resurgence of socialist politics hold some real promise for saving humanity and our feverish planet. If nothing else, they prove that people can, and will, stand up to all the money in the world. As the great Indian independence leader Mahatma Gandhi wrote, "Capitalists were after all few in number. The workers were many. But capital was well organized and had learnt to combine. If labor realized its inherent strength and the secret of combination it would rule capital instead of being ruled by it."[3]

The secret is out! Let's see how it can be used to help fight the ruling class of the twenty-first century.

Well-Red

People across the board, especially younger people, are questioning the way the economic system works, confronting enormous challenges like the rise of incredible student loan debt, shrinking support from the social safety net, falling real incomes (and indeed life expectancies), and above all the existential threat of global climate change. These daunting challenges have led young people to question the status quo economic system significantly more than previous US generations, at least according to what they say.

This trend eventuated a series of public opinion polls over the last several years that have created quite a stir among liberals and conservatives. Among the increasingly prevalent views that keep Corporate America awake at night are results from the broadly respected Pew Research polling agency. As far back as 2014, Pew observed that two-thirds of Americans recognized that economic inequality had grown, and with little difference between political party affiliations. And despite no support for the idea in dominant corporate media, in order to reduce poverty "54% of all Americans [supported] raising taxes on the wealthy and corporations in order to expand programs for the poor." Half of respondents said poverty was due to circumstances beyond a person's control, versus 35 percent who blamed a lack of hard work. Half said that the rich owe it to having "more advantages than others." Americans said by two to one that "the economic system unfairly favors the wealthy."[4] And an incredible 66 percent said there were "very strong" or "strong conflicts between the rich and the poor."[5]

By 2016, a Harvard University survey of young adults found that 51 percent did not support capitalism, while 42 percent did. The survey noted, reasonably, that "capitalism" and especially "socialism" are not terms with universally agreed-upon meanings, but still only among respondents over fifty years of age did a majority say it supported capitalism.[6] This began the now-common media story that young people hate capitalism.

To clarify the issue, Pew returned to the subject in 2019 and included in their results the "crosstabs," or views by respondent category. This added some fascinating results, such as that African Americans are the most socialist unit of the United States, with 65 percent having a "very or somewhat positive impression of socialism." Fifty percent of all respondents aged eighteen to twenty-nine said the same, and support for socialism rises as family income falls.[7]

Pew also asked respondents to use their own words to describe what the terms meant to them, and which system they supported most. The 42 percent with a positive view of socialism gave responses to the effect that it "creates a fairer, more generous system" and "builds upon and improves capitalism," while the 55 percent with a negative view in the poll said it "undermines work ethic, increases reliance on government" and referred to "historical and comparative failure." Among the 33 percent with a negative view of capitalism, respondents said the system "benefits only a few/unequal distribution of wealth," and found it "exploitative/corrupt in nature." The 65 percent with a positive view of capitalism found it "promotes individual opportunity" and was "essential to America."[8]

For the record, capitalism is usually defined as an economic system characterized by markets and private property—meaning *productive* private property, like large farms, semiconductor plants, and data centers, rather than petty private property, like your personal clothes and toothbrush. Socialism is usually defined as a system with public or social ownership of productive property and a more equal, or egalitarian, distribution of wealth.

The highly respected Gallup polling agency found the next year that more than half of US Democrats, 57 percent, had a positive view of socialism, with support for capitalism falling from 56 percent in 2016 to 47 percent in 2020.[9] These numbers do move up and down over the short term, but it's worth noting again and again that the US is a hyper-capitalist country with schooling and media that present wall-to-wall support for free markets and capitalism, with private media trumpeting the superiority of free enterprise to Big Government, and schools requiring economics classes with a curriculum that is little more than glorified capitalist indoctrination. And yet the outsourcing tsunami of the last thirty years—and then the years of pandemic lockdown—have unmistakably taught the public they are considered disposable. So what is the best that can be achieved by cradle-to-grave propaganda? Support for the system of about 3:2. Nothing to write home about!

The broad pattern has held up in other polling. Pew found in 2023 that Americans' biggest complaint about taxes was that "some corporations don't pay their fair share" and "some wealthy people don't pay their fair share," both of which were reported more bothersome than the amount respondents personally paid.[10] Axios, the popular short-form news site, ran a survey with pollster Momentive in 2021, finding "just half of younger Americans now hold a positive view of capitalism—and socialism's appeal in the U.S. continues to grow, driven by Black Americans and women," in part due to the effects of the COVID-19 pandemic offering an opportunity for people to "re-evaluate their political and economic worldview." Among the findings were that "just 66% of Republicans and GOP-leaners ages 18–34 have a positive view of capitalism, down from 81% in January 2019," and an incredible "56% of younger Republicans say the government should pursue policies that reduce the wealth gap." Forty-one percent of all adults viewed socialism favorably, and "socialism has positive connotations for 60% of Black Americans, 45% of American women and 33% of non-white Republicans." And those eighteen to thirty-four were "almost evenly split between those who view capitalism positively and those who view it negatively (49% vs. 46%). Two years before, that margin was a gaping 20 points."[11]

Importantly, the 2022 numbers are broken down by wealth ranges, a phenomenally useful measure. As socialist blogger Carl Beijer observed, the common insult on commercial media is that

socialism appeals to a bunch of rich kids, but in reality "the numbers point in the opposite direction: socialism does *best* among
poor voters and *worse* among the middle and upper classes." While
support for socialism in lower-income households was split 45 percent to 45 percent in the poll, only 33 percent of middle-income
respondents and upper-income respondents liked the idea. Mirror-
ing this, support for capitalism climbed to 60 percent in middle-income families and 70 percent for rich ones.[12] Which makes sense of
course, since richer people would have the most to lose with socialism taxing their wealth or confiscating their corporate property.
But the cheap, idiotic slur that socialism is popular among rich kids
is common enough to need this refutation.

All these numbers have sent terror through wealthy and conservative circles. The *Economist*, the UK business magazine, ran
a cover story on "The Rise of Millennial Socialism," and you can
just feel the cold sweat on the face of the editors. They fret that
"socialism is back in fashion . . . Socialism is storming back because it has formed an incisive critique of what has gone wrong in
Western societies . . . [T]he left has focused on inequality, the environment, and how to vest power in citizens rather than elites . . .
Yet, although the reborn left gets some things right, its pessimism
about the modern world goes too far."[13] They insist that capitalism is the system of freedom and liberty, despite creating gigantic
monopolies, hyper-rich billionaires, and frequent financial crashes
right in front of their eyes. Some socialists would counterargue that
it's capitalism that's a threat to freedom, by creating a tiny ruling
class to rule over us and destroy the world—I wrote a book making these arguments myself.[14] The *Economist* admits that the Left's
"answer to 'how to pay for it all' is usually to soak the rich . . . quite
an easy sell in America."[15]

Even Glenn Hubbard is sweating young people's disaffection
with capitalism. The Columbia Graduate School of Business professor was the chairman of the Council of Economic Advisers for
the George W. Bush administration and is considered the author

of the multiple major tax cuts that dramatically enriched the top US households. Hubbard wrote for the *Atlantic* that, to his horror, "Even My Business-School Students Have Doubts About Capitalism," with his MBA pupils saying in class that capitalism leaves people behind and that economists are less brilliant than they like to let on.[16] Smart kids!

Especially crucial, all these impressive figures for socialist views are in a condition of *zero* media support for these ideas. TV news, the major newspapers, and the prominent online news portals are private property with all the interests of their rich owners, from Jeff Bezos to the Disney corporation to Elon Musk. Collis Huntington, the Gilded Age railroad monopolist, said he bought newspapers with the plan to "control or burn" them.[17] If the mass media would provide any reasonable opportunity for these subjects to be debated, it is plausible that support for socialism would be significantly higher. When popular socialist figures like Sanders go on Fox News, an eyebrow-raising number of people in the attending audiences show support, or at least an openness to being persuaded. The fact that these high figures for socialism can be reached with wall-to-wall media opposition is pretty stunning, frankly.

Which brings us to another, related movement that gets little love from the private media industry—labor.

The Laborious Movement

The labor movement has struggled against extremely high odds worldwide, dealing with the inherent power of employers over the workforce. As described in chapter 3, the reality is that the productive property that sustains society belongs to a small number of companies and their rich owners, and people's need for income requires us all to compete for positions working for them. While capital owners and company managers like to paint themselves as virtuous entrepreneurs creating jobs for everyone else, their concentrated ownership puts them in a position of power over us, the workers, and over the government as well. For this reason, companies and their wealthy owners have hated unions like poison, so labor unions are *the* definitive means of resisting the otherwise unchallenged power of the ruling class.

That's why there is an incredibly cruel world history of often-violent repression of workers attempting to organize in order to match organized capital. The standard history of the Gilded Age observes, "In his own factories Rockefeller would permit no collective bargaining, but only 'company unions' in the time-honored relationship of 'obedient servants and good masters.'"[18] Carnegie said of his enormous steel empire, "We have no Union in our works."[19] Capitalists have been bent on breaking unions for as long as they have existed.

One significant, and perhaps unlikely, recent development aiding the uphill struggle of labor organizing was the major changes to the US and world workforces ushered in by COVID-19. The respiratory disease that went on to kill over a million Americans followed the historical pattern of past epidemics in reducing the labor force. Older employees took early retirement, some dropped out to care for sick relatives or children when schools and childcare centers closed, and of course many thousands died. These factors "tightened" the labor market, with fewer applicants for positions across the economy, and thus raised worker bargaining power for the first time since the advent of neoliberalism in the 1980s.

Not everyone is happy about this—the always pro-business *Wall Street Journal* complained that "more workers across a range of industries are going on strike ... while the tight labor market has taken away some of the risk of walking off the job," observing that there were 180 strikes over the first half of 2022, up from 102 a year before, and with three times the number of workers involved.[20] The *New York Times* added that "shortages in labor and supplies ... leave employers more vulnerable," and that while "large companies have considerable power ... the fitful economic recovery from the pandemic has eroded management's advantages." Therefore "companies often pre-empt a labor action by improving compensation," a welcome move to many workers since the class reality is "the mere act of striking can exert an enormous psychological and financial toll in an economy where workers have a limited safety net. When unionized workers receive strike pay, it's typically a fraction of their usual pay, and they must often picket outside their workplace to receive it."[21]

The press reports that in 2022 "68% of Americans approved of labor unions, more than at any other time since 1965." And yet, America's "union density"—the proportion of its workforce represented by a union—fell to 6.1 percent of private employers in 2021.[22] Labor organizing is technically legally protected in the US, but in practice companies can often get away with canning activists. The press reports that after initially humoring organizers, companies like Apple and Starbucks began firing them, usually for flimsy reasons that are contradicted by previous actions, such as firing one employee shortly after promoting them. Apple's Kansas City store fired five active union organizers in 2023, for offenses like tardiness that workers were not previously punished for. A federal judge found Starbucks illegally fired seven employees in the Buffalo area shortly after their union won a pair of elections there.[23]

The already-lopsided reality of US labor law is being made more unbalanced by the month, as when the now notoriously right-wing Supreme Court expanded the exposure of striking workers to liability if their employers' property is at all damaged during a work stoppage.[24] This follows other recent court decisions, including that many workers can't bring collective legal action against employers, that public sector unions can't require nonmembers to pay fees related to collective bargaining, and that unions can't access company property to talk to workers, and many others reviewed in Adam Cohen's *Supreme Inequality*, finding one of the Court's main legacies has been to support corporations, tilt the playing field against unions, and remove even middle-class means to contesting them like class action lawsuits.

By the 2010s, "the evidence showed that the Court's conservative justices were not just pro-business—they were extraordinarily so by historical standards. A study released in 2013 calculated that all five members of the conservative majority at that time . . . were among the top ten most pro-business justices to serve on the Court since 1946 . . . Alito was the single most pro-business justice of the thirty-five who had served since 1946, and Roberts came in second."[25] The Court found time for these ruling-class-friendly rulings while also striking down national abortion access, affirmative action, and protections for gay consumers.

But despite this repression by state and capital, the results of organizing in the aftermath of an epidemic have been fascinating and a source of some hope. West Coast port workers won a major 32 percent pay increase in 2023, as well as a onetime "hero bonus" honoring the dozens of dockworkers who died while keeping the ports running during COVID. Other transportation-related workers have also won significant improvements, like a 30 percent bump in pay and pension contributions for FedEx pilots, and 34 percent raises for pilots at Delta Air Lines and Spirit.[26]

Often this wave of workplace actions is more about work conditions than pay. Seven hundred Pennsylvanian nursing home employees struck successfully for raises, but also ceilings for patient-to-nurse ratios. Two thousand mental health therapists at the Kaiser Permanente system in California and Hawaii struck for pay increases, and for Kaiser to reduce the wait for patient appointments, which according to the union could take eight weeks or longer.[27]

Other actions have been met with setbacks. Rail workers, for example, have been horribly squeezed by the shrinking number of rail shipping companies since their deregulation in the 1980s. The companies, under Wall Street pressure to cut costs and raise their return on assets, implemented "precision scheduled railroading," which means having only one or two workers operating enormously long trains that may stretch over a mile. To keep to this low-cost model, the railroads required their workers to remain "on call," and to work for days and sometimes weeks on end without conventional weekends or any other regular time off. The lines then added a punitive points system where workers lost points for scheduling days off, even for family events or emergency illness. Running out of points meant suspensions and eventually firings, but the points could be earned back by being on call for two full weeks straight.[28] The rail workers were ready to strike in 2022 to push back on these conditions until President Biden, using national authority over the crucial transport system that ships a giant proportion of goods across the nation, forced a settlement with limited raises but that left the system largely in place.

This upturn during the pandemic has built on gains from before the plague years. Teachers in 2018 engaged in a series of strikes across the US, some wildcat (not authorized by a national union body), taking a full half-million teachers and support staff to the picket lines.[29] Teachers are also endeavoring to organize a national campaign aimed at the growing number of charter schools, which are sensationally popular with conservatives since they are publicly funded but privately run—often by religious groups or billionaires. The *Journal* reports hundreds of charter school teachers in Los Angeles voting to join teachers' unions, desiring "job security and input into the curriculum and other decisions now handed down by administrators and a board that includes Anthony Ressler, a billionaire who bought the Atlanta Hawks [in 2015]."[30]

The effort to organize the coffee chain Starbucks has been a significant beacon of hope. From 2021 to 2023, no fewer than 331 Starbucks locations voted to unionize. In addition to the generally tight labor conditions following the epidemic, the press notes that college-educated workers, often consigned to service work well below their qualifications and saddled with major student loan debt, are increasingly viewing unions favorably. Over 70 percent of college grads support organizing, with even higher numbers among younger workers. The press notes that while typically a minority in "nonprofessional workplaces," workers with a degree often "feel empowered in ways that others don't." The *New York Times* notes a further factor, especially important in the US: "They often know their rights under labor law."[31] On top of these generally favorable views of unions prevailing among the typical barista demographics, the particular conditions at the café chain also have some favorable features, such as long stretches without a shift manager present. This lack of direct oversight allows open discussions about pay and working conditions, something that is especially important for campaigns like these that are led by workers rather than a professional organizer.

While eager to avoid looking too clearly like a union buster, the company has adopted all the conventional anti-union tactics discussed in chapter 3, including the final step—closing. After vague reports of drug-related incidents common in retail settings, Starbucks closed a dozen stores, including two unionized shops in Seattle and one in Portland that had petitioned for recognition.[32] All stores in college town Ithaca, NY were closed amid an organizing drive. So far no unionized Starbucks has a union contract.

Amazon has been a tougher nut to crack. Labor has struggled to make inroads organizing the mammoth online retailer's enormous workforce, which is second only to Walmart in its number of employees. The warehouse workers' union failed to organize a number of Amazon facilities, most prominently an enormous depot in Alabama, losing the vote by large margins after Amazon reached for every union-busting tool in the box. Organizers noted that early in the drive, over two thousand workers signed union cards, but in the end only about a third of that number voted for the union. The *Times* suggested, "The erosion of that early support showed the power that employers have in campaigning against unions by holding mandatory meetings and talking to employees during work hours about the downside of organizing . . . The company's slogan—'Do it without dues'—was pushed to workers in text messages, mandatory meetings and signs in bathroom stalls."[33]

But the organizers won global headlines when a long, tough campaign of two years led to a successful union election at a giant Amazon facility on Staten Island, known in the company as JFK8. Despite celebrated raises, eighteen bucks an hour isn't much in New York, and some workers were homeless, sleeping in their cars in the facility parking lot.[34] Organizers campaigned daily outside the facility, hosting cookouts, recording TikTok videos, and handing out free marijuana to workers. Amazon's attempts to overturn the election ultimately failed, although the company has so far refused to negotiate a contract with the union, a very common corporate tactic to continue dragging out the process and hoping union supporters will get burned out or economically exhausted.[35]

An attempt by the same union, Amazon Labor Union, to organize another Staten Island facility failed, due in part to the challenge of building relationships and solidarity at workplaces with turnover rates in excess of 100 percent a year.[36] Another vote at a facility in upstate New York failed as well, after Amazon said the company held mandatory meetings with employees to help them "understand the facts."[37]

Elsewhere in tech, a few Apple retail stores have voted in a new union, pleasingly called the Apple Coalition of Organized Retail Employees. Apple, as noted above, humored the organizers at first in order to maintain its progressive corporate persona, but now that some have succeed it's taken a more aggressive stance toward organizers by finding ways to shitcan worker-leaders.[38] Tesla workers in Buffalo are attempting to win collective bargaining, fighting an uphill battle against celebrated tech imbecile Elon Musk. Musk has disparaged unions and been found by the National Labor Relations Board to have illegally fired a worker supportive of organizing in a Fremont, California plant. It also found Musk "illegally threatened workers with the loss of stock options if they unionized."[39]

The gigantic tech monopolist Microsoft now has its own first employees represented by a union after a video game studio, which the trillion-dollar platform company acquired in its gaming push, voted for representation with the Communications Workers of America. Under heavy regulatory scrutiny in the deal, Microsoft grudgingly agreed to remain neutral through the union campaign and spared employees the usual mandatory anti-union meetings and messaging.[40] It will supposedly also remain neutral if employees pursue unionization at Activision Blizzard, if its acquisition of the gaming giant is finalized.

These promising early victories are small though compared to the successful United Auto Workers strike in 2023, a large inspiring triumph after decades of union concessions to the automakers like health care and pensions cuts, and the creation of two-tiered contracts paying new hires less. By negotiating with all three US car majors at once while striking individual high-value workplaces one at a time, the autoworkers employed a powerful strategy that in weeks mounted the disruption until the companies gave in. The tentative contract would eliminate the tier system, mandate real raises that by 2028 will see workers earning in the $80,000s a year, and importantly include a provision for company-funded strike pay.[41] The new union leadership is far more dynamic and radical than the previous corrupt senior figures, and is openly encouraging other unions to align their own contract negotiations with it in future years to multiply the strength of the movement.[42]

That's a road trip you'd actually enjoy being on.

Company Frowns

But in the face of these positive developments, employers are still endeavoring to turn back the clock, including bringing back a very traditional means of controlling the workforce—the company town. Referring to urban settlements fully dominated by one employer (and often founded by and controlled by that employer), company towns have a bad reputation for exploiting the workers not just on the clock like usual, but in their every commercial transaction and indeed almost every human activity. The company town is considered to be a symbol of the ultimate exploitation of workers, with the potential for wide surveillance and the increased power of a boss who can not only fire you but evict you on the same day. Company towns are today seen as a relic, but they are most definitely making a comeback, and are surprisingly similar to their earlier analogs from the Gilded Age of hyperconcentrated wealth.

Classic cases include Krupp, the great German munitions company famous for supplying the Reich with the weapons to fight various world wars. During the 1890s Alfred Krupp oversaw incredible growth in his business, to the point that new housing was needed around the giant industrial city of Essen. Krupp built several new suburbs or "colonies," as John Kampfner describes in *The Rich*:

> Krupp arranged his city according to the needs of the business. Rents in company homes were up to 20 per cent cheaper than those for private rooms in town; this was designed to tie in his labourers. The policy at least had the merit of transparency: a new worker was told that if he left the firm for another job, he would lose his accommodation. His rent came straight out of his wage packet and went back into the company. He would spend his money in the Krupp stores . . . The transformation of Essen into a company town was complete by the mid-1870s . . . Krupp's dream was for workers to spend their lives from cradle to grave in the control of the company. [43]

He said, "We only want loyal men, who are grateful to us in their hearts and lives for giving them their daily bread."

The model is a mainstay of capitalism, and many US cities, like Gary, Indiana, were founded as company towns under the utter tyranny of the boss. One case under development today is the brainchild of Musk, the famous tech incompetent. Various corporate entities connected to Musk's staff and companies are buying extensive tracts of ranchland outside Austin, Texas, in order to build a "utopia" on the Colorado River, a location that the *Wall Street Journal* noted would "allow Mr. Musk to set some regulations in his own municipality and expedite his plans." The settlement would have well-below-market rents of $800 a month for Musk's employees, relative to median rents in the county of $2,200 a month. Great deal, except again the reality of having not only your livelihood, but your living quarters under the control of your boss. "If an employee leaves or is fired, he or she would have to vacate the house within 30 days."[44]

Globally, however, companies continue to pursue the cost-cutting method of boosting profit employed since the advent of globalization in the 1980s—capital mobility. This means closing down production in a developed country where workers expect expensive entitlements like health care and moving production somewhere cheaper. China's own development is now driving some manufacturers to yet poorer countries, like Malaysia and Vietnam, especially apparel makers who are most sensitive to labor costs—even China's average labor cost of $3.27 an hour is too much for some firms.[45]

The mobility of capital, where giant global companies belonging to the ruling class can use pro-business policies and free trade agreements to shut down plants and quickly move them across borders, is a wild contrast to the mobility of labor. While firms can move across international frontiers, and international financial networks can send gigantic amounts of liquid wealth breezily around the world, human beings are another story. Sociologist Stanley Aronowitz wrote that "the heart of laborism is that workers, through their unions, are constituted to limit capital's freedom to put labor in competition with itself globally as well as within the nation-state."[46]

Western nations from the EU to the US are regularly consumed with periodic anti-immigrant hysteria (especially funny in immigration-founded countries like the US and Australia), even in the face of the post-COVID labor shortage. This has led to conditions where, since adults are reliably turned away at the US-Mexico border, unaccompanied minors are coming across in significant numbers, creating an opportunity for "sponsors" to bring children from Central America and put them to work paying off the resulting debts, a new form of indentured servitude, mostly for child labor.

Thus the news services have found extensive use of undocumented child labor, for example in the US auto parts supply chain, especially for Korean automaker Hyundai. They report that when Labor Department inspectors arrived without notice at one plant, "workers rushed out the back and left the premises before they could be questioned." Hyundai claimed it would cut off those suppliers, but later backed off the claim. Reuters adds, "In two separate statements sent by the same public relations firm, [the Hyundai contractors] said their policies forbid the hiring of any workers not of legally employable age. Using identical language, both companies said they hadn't, 'to the best of our knowledge,' hired underage workers."[47]

The *Times* reported on a Grand Rapids, Michigan, plant for Hearthside Food Solutions—which produces and packages processed food for huge brands like Cheetos, Lucky Charms, and Nature Valley granola bars—where workers under sixteen worked on dangerous fast-moving assembly lines during twelve-hour shifts. The paper found "twelve-year-old roofers in Florida and Tennessee. Underage slaughterhouse workers in Delaware, Mississippi and North Carolina . . . In town after town, children scrub dishes late at night. They run milking machines in Vermont and deliver meals in New York City . . . Girls as young as 13 wash hotel sheets in Virginia . . . [M]iddle and high school teachers in English-language learner programs say it is now common for nearly all their students to rush off to long shifts after their classes end."[48]

The great labor journal *Labor Notes* wrote of the trend, "That's how billionaires become billionaires—by cutting corners on safety, forcing us to work at unsafe speeds, and not paying us for the full value of the work we do." It cites a report of a thirteen-year-old working nights at a slaughterhouse, "A school nurse learned about the girl's night job after finding 'chemical burns, blisters and open wounds on her hands and one knee.'"[49]

But it's not just immigrant youths—states across the US are loosening century-old child labor laws. The *Journal* reports that Georgia, Ohio, Missouri, South Dakota, Illinois, New Jersey, and New Hampshire have lengthened the number of hours fourteen- and fifteen-year-olds can work, or removed the need for a company to get a government permit to employ kids under sixteen. Work hours for that age group are still limited by federal law on school nights, and it still bars them from certain dangerous work. But the US Labor Department found a 69 percent increase in minors found to be illegally employed since 2018.[50]

Conservatives are applauding these changes—the right-wing *Wall Street Journal* editorial page wrote, "A Little Work Never Hurt Anyone—Including Teenagers," an impressive claim, considering the literal crushing in construction and dismemberment in meat-packing that are too often reported by these kids. The editorial claims, "Opponents of these state laws are carrying water for Big Labor. The goal is not protecting children. Rather, it's protecting the pay of current employees by restricting the supply of labor."[51] And this is partly true, since child labor laws were partially insti-tuted in the first place to keep adults from having to compete for jobs with poor dumb kids with no knowledge of their rights or worth, and to allow children to focus on school instead of sleeping through it after a night shift.

A revived labor movement will have some junior members indeed.

Berning Point

Part of the reason this lurch back toward Gilded Age working conditions is possible is because labor has few political allies. This likely owes much to the fact that labor's interests are diametrically opposed to business, which has the ultimate political trump card—gigantic amounts of money in a country where getting elected is incredibly expensive. The average Senate race in 2022 cost $13.5 million, and both Joe Biden and Donald Trump spent over a billion dollars apiece on their 2020 campaigns (counting spending by their affiliated political action committees), according to the Center for Responsive Politics.[52]

The gigantic cost of running for office means that most politicians must make extensive promises to donors, who can kick into their campaign accounts and their shadowy PACs. People and institutions with money to contribute are less likely to favor candidates or policies that would tax their wealth or break up their monopolies, so the tendency is that America's popular leftist views, described above, seldom get translated into policies. A recent study used political survey data and a regression method to conclude "senators are vastly more responsive to the views of affluent constituents than to constituents of modest means. For example, constituents at the 75th percentile of the income distribution appear to have almost three times as much influence as those at the 25th percentile on senators' overall voting patterns, and several times as much influence on specific roll call votes. Constituents near the top of the income distribution have even more influence."[53]

And I think we all know how disconnected we tend to feel from our theoretical representatives in state and national capitals. The idea of getting officeholders to aid a constituent sounds immediately unlikely or at least daunting to a lot of politically unserved or cynical people. The political Right seizes on this to advance its claim of the inherent uselessness of government, that it can literally never do anything right, wastes public money to no end, and other incorrect remarks mostly aimed at getting taxes and regulations off the backs of the rich, which they have succeeded at. A more thoughtful approach would recognize we feel we have no control over our representatives not because it's impossible to have a good republic, but because another class of society has all the liquid assets, real property, industrial equity, and media resources to broadly run the private society and be in a position to decisively influence the state. Government really can serve us, but only if we have meaningful democratic control over it, rather than leaving it to secretive ghouls who insist we pay no attention to the man behind the curtain.

So in the present system it's unsurprising that you get more of a hearing if you're a ruling-class citizen, affluent enough to contribute the legal maximum to national political campaigns and throw fundraising parties for the candidates. Indeed, if you're rich enough you can take sitting US Supreme Court justices out on fancy international beach trips and long jaunts on your superyacht, as was scandalously revealed to be the basis of the relationship between billionaire real estate developer Harlan Crow and archconservative justice Clarence Thomas (who also forgot to file any of the legally required disclosures about these regular "gifts").[54] The ultimate in access is to be rich enough to host some of the most powerful men in the world on your pleasure boats, and have whatever political conversation you want away from prying eyes.

Beyond the gigantic cost, leftist politicians get an additional level of unsurprising hostility from commercial media and their corporate or billionaire owners. In particular, the surprisingly successful national campaigns of Vermont senator Bernie Sanders have encountered truly adversarial media, for example in the *Wall Street Journal*, property of Australian archconservative world media billionaire Rupert Murdoch. The *Journal* grudgingly admitted that "socialism appears to carry far less of a stigma than it once did, particularly among young people who form the base of Mr. Sanders's support," noting a *Boston Globe* poll finding fully 31 percent of Democratic primary voters in New Hampshire said the term "socialist" described their political views.[55] It noted too that this was inconceivable before the monumental financial crash of 2008 and the resulting Occupy Wall Street movement of 2011, which opened up many people to a recognition that capitalism may not be the very final form of human social organization. And the media hostility was almost uniform, with all major cable and broadcast news channels openly rooting against the popular candidate.

Seattle voters elected socialist economist Kshama Sawant to the city council in 2013, after she ran on a proposal to significantly raise the city's minimum wage in order for workers to keep up with the rising cost of living. This was a shock to the business world, accustomed to more pliant liberal politicians (although Seattle had elected a socialist mayor as recently as 1922).[56] Not content to simply raise the wage floor while the owning class calls the shots, when hyper-profitable aircraft giant Boeing threatened to relocate production if its main labor union didn't accept major concessions, Sawant argued publicly that "workers should take over the factories and re-tool the machines to produce buses," as business news outlet Bloomberg disgustedly put it.[57]

With the insane expense of running for national office in the US, plus the predictable commercial media hostility, it could be argued that the real point of many socialist campaigns, at this time, is mainly to use elections' brief period of actual national political attention to put socialist ideas in front of the country. Socialist campaigns have been rather successful in this regard, for example with the flagship socialist policy proposal, Medicare for All, which would create a kind of "single-payer" public health system that covers everyone and spares you dealing with insurance corporations ever again. Support for it has grown as Americans have overheard scraps of comparisons with other capitalist countries, like the UK, where the conservative *Financial Times* compared US life expectancy to that of Blackpool, England, well known within the UK as being an extremely poor town with the lowest life expectancy in the kingdom. The *Times* concluded that "the average American now has the same chance of a long and healthy life as someone born in Blackpool, the town with England's lowest life expectancy." Blackpool residents could expect to live five years longer than people in the poorest US communities. More cruelly, "one in 25 American five-year-olds today will not make it to their 40th birthday. No parent should ever have to bury their child, but in the US one set of parents from every kindergarten class most likely will."[58]

Pew found that 63 percent of Americans supported some form of government health care program in 2020 (up from 59 percent the year before), including 34 percent of Republicans and 88 percent of Democrats.[59] This is an incredible achievement, since there is again literally no visible support for this type of program in national media, which of course earn much of their profit from ad spending by health insurers, the pharmaceutical industry, and hospital chains, to whom the idea is like a bone-felt religious taboo.

In addition to important policies like M4A, the Sanders campaigns have had major effects on opening up people to broader political ideas. Carl Beijer notes that a "Bernie Bump" is visible in levels of polled support for socialism, with stated support rising from 35 percent in the Pew polls to 42 percent around the second Sanders campaign in 2020.[60] Sanders is likable and a good communicator, but isn't a singular figure—this bump likely has more to do with Americans being briefly exposed to leftist ideas that the media, for a minute, couldn't ignore as usual.

Beyond current political candidates, the socialist tradition has prominent figures, like the great physicist Albert Einstein. Remembered today as a brilliant scientist and commemorated in cheesy posters worldwide, Einstein is part of a great, long tradition of socialists whose left-wing ideas have been scrubbed from the record. Few students are aware that Einstein wrote an essay for the socialist journal *Monthly Review*, in which he argued,

> The economic anarchy of capitalist society as it exists today is, in my opinion, the real source of the evil . . . Insofar as the

labor contract is "free," what the worker receives is deter-
mined not by the real value of the goods he produces, but
by his minimum needs and by the capitalists' requirements
for labor power in relation to the number of workers competing for jobs . . . Private capital tends to become concentrated in few hands, partly because of competition among
the capitalists, and partly because technological development and the increasing division of labor encourage the
formation of larger units of production at the expense of
smaller ones. The result of these developments is an oligar-
chy of private capital the enormous power of which cannot
be effectively checked even by a democratically organized
political society. This is true since the members of legisla-
tive bodies are selected by political parties, largely financed
or otherwise influenced by private capitalists who, for all
practical purposes, separate the electorate from the legislature . . . Moreover, under existing conditions, private capitalists inevitably control, directly or indirectly, the main
sources of information (press, radio, education). It is thus
extremely difficult, and indeed in most cases quite impossible, for the individual citizen to come to objective conclusions and to make intelligent use of his political rights . . . I
am convinced there is only *one* way to eliminate these grave
evils, namely through the establishment of a socialist economy, accompanied by an educational system which would
be oriented toward social goals. In such an economy, the
means of production are owned by society itself and are uti-
lized in a planned fashion.[61]

Or take Martin Luther King, discussed in chapter 3 as a great
ally of the labor movement, and who is commemorated on the level
of a secular saint for his nonviolent approach to racial justice. Like
many progressive and radical Black intellectuals, King had little
confidence in capitalism. He wrote in a letter to his future wife

that "I am much more socialistic in my economic theory than cap-
italistic," adding that "capitalism has outlived its usefulness." He
later told the national press of his work with the Southern Christian Leadership Conference, "In a sense, you could say we are engaged in the class struggle," and said at an SCLC staff retreat that
perhaps "America must move toward a democratic socialism."[62] A
seldom-mentioned part of King's legacy.

Another socialist, the UK writer George Orwell, is famous for
his great satires of the totalitarianism of allegedly socialist states
like the Soviet Union in his books *1984* and *Animal Farm*. But it's
pretty cheap that we very infrequently hear that he also said things
like "Every line of serious work that I have written since 1936 has
been written, directly or indirectly, *against* totalitarianism and *for*
democratic socialism, as I understand it."[63] Among his extensive
writing in support of socialist movements, he elaborated that "The
only thing *for* which we can combine is the underlying ideal of Socialism: justice and liberty."[64]

The full nature and history of socialism require their own
book. I'll get around to it! For now, it's essential to keep in mind
how popular these ideas remain even when fully locked out of commercial media, popular education, and the bipartisan political consensus. Some ideas are too sensible and popular to bury completely.

But we should take a moment to reflect on what socialism
would mean. The traditional socialist goals—rough economic
equality and worker control of the means of production—require
the end of private ownership of large-scale property. Not your personal things, but the manufacturing plants, data centers, and great
industrial capital that make up the productive economy. Presently
those enormous assets are the private property of individuals or
companies and their stockholders, and thus pursue market goals of
maximized profitability.

So inevitably, socialism would require the end of private
ownership of the productive economy. That means *expropriation*,
taking these assets away from their present hyper-rich owners.

Much like the slave economy in the nineteenth century or local fire stations in the twentieth, these assets *should* be taken away from the rich, and run through different forms of public management, accountable to a democratic process. Everyone likes those historic expropriations, and now we just need a final great one to end all the endless nightmares and abjectly intolerable social outcomes this book has reviewed.

There is no social battle that would be harder. Expropriation is (rightly) recognized by the rich as the ultimate threat to them, and anytime someone proposes some relatively mild tax increase or other burden on them, they immediately suggest the tax is the First Step to Socialism and the expropriation of their monumental wealth. And because the media remain private property, their message will be loud enough to resonate widely.

But we should ask ourselves, why were the rich able to bring about the turn back toward unregulated markets and low taxes that we call neoliberalism? It's because the reforms of European social democracy and the US New Deal did not expropriate the rich—while heavily taxed and subject to extensive public regulation, private property remained private and our oligarchs remained our oligarchs. Wall Street, big industry, the military contractors, the early tech industry—those giant institutions remained the property of rich individuals or, more commonly, enormous corporations owned by rich individuals. Their large-scale private property endured all the burdens and indignities of the short social democratic era of the Western world, created by long-running movements that climaxed during the Great Depression, but powered by human beings, not immortal corporate institutions.

And once people wearied of the problems of the era, private media could frame the issues as the result of too much Big Government, and get popular support behind figures like US president Reagan, UK prime minister Thatcher, and related shady characters in business and finance who ran the neoliberal push to return to the total playground for the rich that was the Gilded Age—all too successfully.

Should our current movement succeed and inaugurate a new period of labor organization and socialist political gains, we must not repeat the same mistake. Any future success by socialists will be met with resisting cries not to go too far, just let the clever corporate managers run the transition to a democratic-run economy, don't throw out the benefits of free markets in the revolution. But those free markets don't make us free to consume the abundant wealth, and those clever managers will inevitably be looking for opportunities to set the process back and return their former private paymasters to their positions of rule.

The single way to avoid this fatal error is to commit to a program of expropriation as a core element of future socialist politics. This—this simple idea—is the foundation stone for any future we might hope for with basic economic security for our kids and any chance of an inhabitable future natural environment.

We live in a world with millions of homeless citizens even as the rich hoard thousands of properties sitting empty, of ugly concrete warehouses that hold humanity's artistic and cultural treasures while they inflate someone's asset portfolio, of privately owned fossil fuel–burning power plants dooming us all daily. Working people should be living in those properties, the art and artifacts should be in museums, and that energy system should be going through a crash conversion to renewables. It's hard to see that happening without a real socialist movement, and indeed a thorough-enough change to no longer be considered a reform— socialism and solutions to our problems require a real revolution.

Assets like computer processor chip fabricators, chemicals plants, utility networks, and enormous agricultural estates should not belong to one person, or one corporation. They should be the property of common humanity, should be run democratically, and should contribute to a world of equality and sustainability.

Anything less, and the same completely mad capitalist system will remain, with elites a step away from returning to power and an economy slowly, steadily killing the planet's biosphere.

Better the scary uncertainty of fundamental change than the certainty of destroying the world. No one wants to live in such turbulent times as these, but creating a free, socialist future is an unmatchable gift we could give to coming generations.

Steal from the rich and give to the poor, sounds like a winner.

Class Dismissed

For all its popular support, the labor movement still frequently loses, and progressive candidates often go down in defeat. Polling support for socialism and broad approval of labor unions are great, but turning them into actual social change takes struggle, trying and failing and learning from mistakes. It's hard to compete with giant corporate networks able to move jobs around countries and the world, oceans' worth of shadowy cash drowning out socialist candidates, and wall-to-wall corporate ownership of media, meaning the sources we use to learn about the world remain the property of the ruling class.

But centuries of the rule of gold shouldn't discourage us. Few expected the giant events and upheavals of this era, from epidemics to wars to bank panics. And few people thought that past systems of power and wealth could be fundamentally changed, that the French revolutionaries could overthrow the king or that the US slaveholding aristocracy could have its human property pried from its grip. If the penniless citizens of Haiti could throw out their imperial overlords, if workers could organize a drive for universal health care in a country as business-run as Britain, if a leftist could get the message of popular socialist policies on TV before millions of people, there is real hope that humanity can move beyond capitalism. Some people don't care for this idea, but it's plain historical fact that all our positive social changes and victories for oppressed

people seldom come from fits of conscience among the powerful—
they come from broad movements of social struggle where people
turn out for demonstrations, strikes, meetings, and organizing actions over years.

People are ready to fight back. A recent poll found an overwhelming majority of Americans are pessimistic about the future
and that of their children, with 44 percent saying their financial
situation is worse than they expected for their stage in life.[65] The
BBC recently reported that the UK Red Cross is organizing a food
aid campaign for Britain, which has seen a huge rise in demand for
food aid since the Conservative government instituted austerity
programs that included cuts to public support, along with similar
programs in the EU. The Red Cross, which had not operated food
aid in the UK since World War II, said this move had been accompanied by a half million people needing food bank support in Britain, along with a 75 percent increase in demand for food aid on the
continent.[66] Bloomberg reported in spring 2023, with a tight job
market and a growing economy, that the line for the American Red
Cross Food Pantry in Boston was the length of two football fields.[67]

Back when the US invaded Iraq without justification, millions of people flooded into the streets of the world's cities in ur-
gent opposition. The upsurge of popular activism led the staid *New
York Times* to declare, "There may still be two superpowers on
the planet: the United States and world public opinion."[68] When
French president Emmanuel Macron, after a bitter fight, overrode
large majorities and raised the retirement age even while cutting
taxes on the rich, protesters stormed the headquarters of the
French luxury goods conglomerate LVMH, the CEO of which,
Bernard Arnault, was the world's richest man at the time. Demon-
strators chanted, "There is money in the pockets of billionaires."[69]
It's no lie—*Bloomberg* reported the world's richest five hundred
people added $852 billion to their fortunes in the first half of 2023
alone, with each member of its Billionaires Index gaining an average of $14 million—a *day*.[70]

The editor-in-chief of the *Wall Street Journal* himself, Gerard Baker, wrote that today "Aristocrats Face the Pitchforks," observing that "life's winners" gathering in elite circles like the World Economic Forum are disconnected from the struggles of the global majority. He goes on, referring to the infamous ruling regimes of France and Russia before their revolutions: "The history of aristocracies has mostly ended unhappily . . . [T]he best they may be able to hope for is a less violent, less terminal, but ultimately no less significant modern-day version of what happened to the Bourbons or the Romanovs."[71]

Olúfẹmi O. Táíwò wrote in his book *Elite Capture* that for all of today's long overdue appreciation for racial diversity and land acknowledgments, "no matter who we 'center' in our organizing culture's thoughts and messages, there will be lead in our water until and unless we do something about the pipes."[72] The escaped slave and self-taught intellectual Frederick Douglass said, "The whole history of the progress of human liberty shows that all concessions yet made to her august claims have been born of earnest struggle . . . If there is no struggle there is no progress."[73]

In all its forms around the world, the struggle against today's ruling class will decide what kind of future humanity and the Earth will have. Let's fight for a good one, because if we don't, a dark one is guaranteed. Ruling classes look invincible right up until they collapse. Maybe your contribution will be a tipping point.

And when struggling against the ruling class, remember to always have a laugh at their expense. They can afford it.

ACKNOWLEDGMENTS

This little book could never have been prepared without the help of many people. The scholars at the World Inequality Database, whose work I've drawn on extensively, are a gift to economists around the world. My Haymarket editor, John McDonald, was as patient as ever with my deadline delays and excessive adverbs. Without the marketing skills and experience of Rory Fanning and Jim Plank, I doubt many people would have seen this book. Of course, all errors, omissions, oversights, and general ham-fisted fuckups are my responsibility.

NOTES

1. John Kampfner, *The Rich: From Slaves to Super Yachts: A 2,000-Year History* (London: Little, Brown, 2014), xi.
2. Matthew Josephson, *The Robber Barons: The Classic Account of the Influential Capitalists Who Transformed America's Future* (New York: Harcourt, 1934), 364.
3. George Orwell, *The Road to Wigan Pier* (Orlando, FL: Harcourt, 1958), 216.

Boss Fight

1. David Streitfeld and Erin Woo, "The Amazonification of Space Begins in Earnest," *New York Times*, July 21, 2021.
2. Tom Wolfe, "Greenwich Time," *New York Times*, September 27, 2008; Daniel Trotta, "'Masters of the Universe' Get Lesson in Humility," Reuters, September 19, 2008.
3. Ajay Kapur, Niall Macleod, and Narendra Singh, "Plutonomy: Buying Luxury, Explaining Global Imbalances," Citigroup, October 16, 2005; Ajay Kapur et al., "The Global Investigator: The Plutonomy Symposium—Rising Tides Lifting Yachts," Citigroup, September 29, 2006.
4. Facundo Alvaredo et al., *World Inequality Report 2018* (World Inequality Lab, 2018), 237; Lucas Chancel et al., *World Inequality Report 2022* (World Inequality Lab, 2021), 251.
5. Sabrina Tavernise and Abby Goodnough, "American Life Expectancy Rises for First Time in Four Years," *New York Times*, January 30, 2020; Alex Lemonides, "While Life Expectancy Is Rebounding in Parts of the World, White Deaths Drive a Further U.S. Drop," *New York Times*, April 9, 2022.
6. Americans for Tax Fairness, "Billionaire Pandemic Wealth Gains of 55%, or $1.6 Trillion, Come Amid Three Decades of Rapid Wealth Growth," Institute for Policy Studies, April 14, 2021.
7. James Morgan, "Rip van Winkle's New World Order," *Financial Times*, April 25, 1992.
8. Peter Wilson, "Want a Second Passport? Try Buying a House," *New York Times*, May 21, 2019.

9.   Peter Bernstein and Annalyn Swan, *All the Money in the World: How the Forbes 400 Make—and Spend—Their Fortunes* (New York: Knopf, 2007), 188.

Introduction: Why Read about the Ruling Class

1.   Deborah Hardoon, "An Economy for the 99%," Oxfam International, January 16, 2017. The paper derives this point from Credit Suisse data and *Forbes*.
2.   Luke Savage, "America's Dynastic Superrich Are Rigging the Rules to Protect Their Power," *Jacobin*, June 16, 2021.
3.   Edward Wolff, "Household Wealth Trends in the United States, 1962 to 2016: Has Middle Class Wealth Recovered?," National Bureau of Economic Research Working Paper No. 24085, November 2017, 16, 37.
4.   Robert Frank, "Why the Rich Like to Eat Gold," *Wall Street Journal*, January 16, 2009.
5.   Julian Guthrie, "Larry Ellison's Fantasy Island," *Wall Street Journal*, June 13, 2013.
6.   Joe Fassler, "The Superyachts of Billionaires Are Starting to Look a Lot Like Theft," *New York Times*, April 10, 2023; Kevin Koenig, "How Much Does That Oligarch's Yacht Actually Cost?," *New York Times*, September 2, 2022.
7.   Lucas Chancel et al., *World Inequality Report 2022* (World Inequality Lab, 2021), 133.
8.   Ben Eisen, "In Coronavirus Recession, the Out-of-Work Turn to GoFundMe," *Wall Street Journal*, November 21, 2020.

Chapter 1: The Numbers

1.   Robert Frank, *Richistan: A Journey Through the 21st Century Wealth Boom and the Lives of the New Rich* (New York: Random House, 2007), 209.
2.   Peter Bernstein and Annalyn Swan, *All the Money in the World: How the Forbes 400 Make—and Spend—Their Fortunes* (New York: Knopf, 2007), 280.
3.   Paul Fussell, *Class: A Guide Through the American Status System* (New York: Simon & Schuster, 1983), 15.
4.   Michael Norton and Dan Ariely, "Building a Better America—One Wealth Quintile at a Time," *Perspectives on Psychological Sciences* 6, no. 1 (January 2011).
5.   Thomas Piketty, *Capital in the Twenty-First Century* (Cambridge, MA: Belknap Press, 2014), 225.
6.   Piketty, *Capital*, 280.
7.   Piketty, *Capital*, 199–201.
8.   Piketty, *Capital*, 301.
9.   Carter Price and Kathryn Edwards, "Trends in Income from 1979 to 2018," RAND Corporation, November 20, 2020.
10. Michael Brill et al., "Understanding the Labor Productivity and Compensation Gap," *Beyond the Numbers* 6, no. 6, (June 2017).
11. Steve Fraser, *The Age of Acquiescence: The Life and Death of American*

Resistance to Organized Wealth and Power (New York: Basic Books, 2015), 66.

12. Piketty, *Capital*, 347–48.

13. Facundo Alvaredo et al., *World Inequality Report 2018* (World Inequality Lab, 2018), 238.

14. Alvaredo et al., *World Inequality Report 2018*, 270, 247.

15. Alvaredo et al., *World Inequality Report 2018*, 238.

16. World Inequality Database, https://wid.world/.

17. Alvaredo et al., *World Inequality Report 2018*, 223.

18. Hibah Yousuf, "Obama Admits 95% of Income Gains Gone to Top 1%," CNN, September 15, 2013.

19. Lucas Chancel et al., *World Inequality Report 2022* (World Inequality Lab, 2021), 96.

20. Alvaredo et al., *World Inequality Report 2018*, 232.

21. Chancel et al., *World Inequality Report 2022*, 251.

22. Chancel et al., *World Inequality Report 2022*, 99.

23. Chancel et al., *World Inequality Report 2022*, 33.

24. Emmanuel Saez and Gabriel Zucman, "The Rise of Income and Wealth Inequality in America: Evidence from Distributional Macroeconomic Accounts," *Journal of Economic Perspectives* 34, no. 4 (Fall 2020): 3–26.

25. Emmanuel Saez, "Striking It Richer: The Evolution of Top Incomes in the United States (Updated with 2018 Estimates)," UC Berkeley, February 2020, Table 1.

26. Bernstein and Swan, *All the Money*, 4.

27. Piketty, *Capital*, 259.

28. Daniel Gilbert, *Stumbling on Happiness* (London: Harper Perennial, 2007), 217–18.

29. Piketty, *Capital*, 391-93.

30. Piketty, *Capital*, 395–96.

31. Piketty, *Capital*, 244, 246.

32. Luke Savage, "America's Dynastic Superrich Are Rigging the Rules to Protect Their Power," *Jacobin*, June 16, 2021.

33. Bloomberg Billionaire Index, https://www.bloomberg.com/billionaires/.

34. Chancel et al., *World Inequality Report 2022*, 15.

35. Rob Larson, *Capitalism vs. Freedom: The Toll Road to Serfdom* (Alresford, UK: Zero Books, 2018), ch. 1 and 2.

36. Kevin A. Hassett and Aparna Mathur, "Hassett and Mathur: Consumption and the Myths of Inequality," *Wall Street Journal*, October 24, 2012.

37. Douglas McWilliams, *The Inequality Paradox: How Capitalism Can Work for Everyone* (New York: Overlook Press, 2018), 27, 33.

38. McWilliams, *Inequality Paradox*, 67.

39. Found at https://www.federalreserve.gov/releases/z1/dataviz/dfa/index.html.

40. Nitasha Tiku and Jay Greene, "The Billionaire Boom," *Washington Post*, March 12, 2021.

41. Americans for Tax Fairness, "Billionaire Pandemic Wealth Gains of 55%,

or $1.6 Trillion, Come Amid Three Decades of Rapid Wealth Growth," Institute for Policy Studies, April 14, 2021.

42. Alvaredo et al., *World Inequality Report 2018*, 240.

43. Norton and Ariely, "Building a Better America."

44. Matt Bruenig, "The Top 1 Percent Owns Nearly Everything in the US. We Need to Seize Their Wealth," *Jacobin*, October 6, 2020.

45. Chancel et al., *World Inequality Report 2022*, 21–22.

46. Chancel et al., *World Inequality Report 2022*, 10–11.

47. Chancel et al., *World Inequality Report 2022*, 269.

48. Chancel et al., *World Inequality Report 2022*, 30.

49. Chancel et al., *World Inequality Report 2022*, 213.

50. Li Shi, Hiroshi Sato, and Terry Sicular, *Rising Inequality in China: Challenges to a Harmonious Society* (Cambridge, MA: Cambridge University Press, 2013), 31.

51. Chancel et al., *World Inequality Report 2022*, 5.

52. Rob Larson, "The IMF's Bottomless Bottom-Line Cruelty," *Current Affairs*, July–August 2021.

53. Chancel et al., *World Inequality Report 2022*, 34, 219.

54. Piketty, *Capital*, 159.

55. Stanley Aronowitz, *How Class Works: Power and Social Movement* (New Haven, CT: Yale University, 2003), 4.

56. Edward Wolff, "Who Owns Stock in American Corporations?," *Proceedings of the American Philosophical Society* 158, no. 4 (December 2014): 383.

57. Wolff, "Who Owns Stock?," 385.

58. Edward Wolff, "Household Wealth Trends in the United States, 1962 to 2016: Has Middle Class Wealth Recovered?," National Bureau of Economic Research Working Paper No. 24085, November 2017, 16, 37.

59. Wolff, "Household Wealth Trends," 18–19.

60. Wolff, "Who Owns Stock?," 380.

61. Piketty, *Capital*, 260.

62. Ed Ford, "Concentration of Stock Ownership," *Dollars & Sense*, (Jan/Feb 2022).

63. Patricia Cohen, "We All Have a Stake in the Stock Market, Right? Guess Again," *New York Times*, February 8, 2018.

64. Robert Frank, "The Wealthiest 10% of Americans Own a Record 89% of All U.S. Stocks," CNBC, October 18, 2021.

65. Theo Francis, "Price Increases Come Easily for Big Businesses, but Inflation Still Squeezes Profits," *Wall Street Journal*, October 10, 2022.

66. Caitlin McCabe, "Companies Are Flush with Cash—and Ready to Pad Shareholder Pockets," *Wall Street Journal*, May 16, 2021.

67. Hannah Miao, "Corporate Stock Buybacks Help Keep Market Afloat," *Wall Street Journal*, February 27, 2023.

68. C. Wright Mills, *The Power Elite* (New York: Oxford University Press, 1956), 122.

69. Igor Makarov and Antoinette Schoar, "Blockchain Analysis of the Bitcoin Market," National Bureau of Economic Research Working Paper 29396, October 2021; Paul Vigna, "Bitcoin's 'One Percent' Controls Lion's Share of the Cryptocurrency's Wealth," *Wall Street Journal*, December 20, 2021.

Chapter 2: The Lifestyle

1. Robert Frank, *Richistan: A Journey Through the 21st Century Wealth Boom and the Lives of the New Rich* (New York: Random House, 2007), 129.
2. Rory Satran, "What the World's Richest People Wear on Yachts," *Wall Street Journal*, August 19, 2023.
3. Thorstein Veblen, *The Theory of the Leisure Class* (Oxford, UK: Oxford University Press, 2007), 26, 29.
4. Veblen, *Theory*, 36–37.
5. Veblen, *Theory*, 41–42.
6. Peter Bearman, *Doormen* (Chicago: University of Chicago Press, 2005), 139, 147.
7. Matthew Dalton, "Luxury Firms Lavish Even More Attention on the Ultrarich," *Wall Street Journal*, March 15, 2017.
8. Robert Frank, "Why the Rich Are Bad Customers," *Wall Street Journal*, September 8, 2010.
9. James Stewart, "The Birthday Party," *New Yorker*, February 4, 2008.
10. Michael de la Merced, "Inside Stephen Schwarzman's Birthday Bash," *New York Times*, February 14, 2007.
11. Thomas Heath, "A Billionaire, Gwen Stefani and a Horde of Camels Bolster the Trump Economy," *Washington Post*, February 15, 2017.
12. Robert Frank, "Why the Rich Like to Eat Gold," *Wall Street Journal*, January 16, 2009.
13. Frank, *Richistan*, 115.
14. Chrystia Freeland, *Plutocrats: The Rise of the New Global Super-Rich and the Fall of Everyone Else* (New York: Penguin, 2013), 6.
15. Nathan Robinson, "How Billionaires See Themselves," *Current Affairs*, January 5, 2021.
16. Arwa Mahdawi, "How Can You Comfort a Sad, Scared Billionaire? Call Them a 'Person of Wealth,'" *Guardian*, April 11, 2023.
17. Veblen, *Theory*, 66–67.
18. Kate Wagner, "You Can't Even Tell Who's Rich Anymore," *Nation*, March 24, 2023.
19. Veblen, *Theory*, 92.
20. Paul Fussell, *Class: A Guide Through the American Status System* (New York: Simon & Schuster, 1983), 30.
21. Peter Bernstein and Annalyn Swan, *All the Money in the World: How the Forbes 400 Make—and Spend—Their Fortunes* (New York: Knopf, 2007), 207–9.
22. Bernstein and Swan, *All the Money*, 223–24.

23. John Kampfner, *The Rich: From Slaves to Super Yachts: A 2,000-Year History* (London: Little, Brown, 2014), 227.

24. Paul Street, *They Rule: The 1% vs. Democracy* (New York: Routledge, 2014), 175–76.

25. Steven Gaines, *Fool's Paradise: Players, Poseurs, and the Culture of Excess in South Beach* (New York: Random House, 2009), 187.

26. Trefor Moss, "Luxury Brands Are Making Watches Even Fewer People Can Afford," *Wall Street Journal*, June 11, 2022.

27. Christina Passariello, "Apple's First Foray into Luxury with Hermès Watch Breaks Tradition," *Wall Street Journal*, September 11, 2015.

28. Aaron Johnson, "Billionaire Melinda Gates Had 'Military Operation' Level Security Protection for 'Today' Show Appearance," Radar Online, May 17, 2023.

29. Julie Creswell, "With Fortune Falling, a 1 Percent Divorce," *New York Times*, February 1, 2014.

30. Nicholas Kulish et al., "The Gateses' Public Split Spotlights a Secretive Fortune," *New York Times*, May 13, 2021.

31. Candace Taylor, "A High-Stakes Divorce Illustrates How the Rich Play Real-Estate Tug of War," *Wall Street Journal*, April 9, 2020.

32. Frank, *Richistan*, 220–21.

33. Nick Kostov and Stacy Meichtry, "The World's Richest Person Auditions His Five children to Run LVMH, the Luxury Empire," *Wall Street Journal*, April 19, 2023.

34. Freeland, *Plutocrats*, 239.

35. Joseph Bernstein, "Elon Musk Has the World's Strangest Social Calendar," *New York Times*, October 11, 2022.

36. Rob Copeland, "The Rich, Famous and In-Between Vie for Elon Musk's Attention," *Wall Street Journal*, September 30, 2022.

37. Clay Cockrell, "I'm a Therapist to the Super-Rich: They Are as Miserable as *Succession* Makes Out," *Guardian*, November 22, 2021.

38. Gaines, *Fool's Paradise*, 158.

39. Nina Munk, "Greenwich's Outrageous Fortune," *Vanity Fair*, July 2006.

40. Katherine Clarke, "With $250 Million Ask, A Storied Bel-Air Estate Becomes America's Priciest Home," *Wall Street Journal*, June 21, 2023.

41. Katherine Clarke, "Decades After Larry Ellison Landed, These Kingpins Are Sending Malibu Real Estate Even Higher," *Wall Street Journal*, June 16, 2022.

42. Julian Guthrie, "Larry Ellison's Fantasy Island," *Wall Street Journal*, June 13, 2013.

43. Katherine Clarke, "Bill and Melinda Gates Buy Oceanfront Home Near San Diego for $43 Million," *Wall Street Journal*, April 21, 2020.

44. Laurence Darmiento, "L.A.'s Most Extravagant Mansion Sells for Less Than Half Its List Price," *Los Angeles Times*, March 3, 2022.

45. Candace Jackson, "Who Wants to Buy the Most Expensive House in America?," *New York Times*, December 23, 2017.

46. Nikita Stewart and David Gelles, "The $238 Million Penthouse, and the Hedge Fund Billionaire Who May Rarely Live There," *New York Times*, January 24, 2019.

47. Britney Nguyen, "See Inside the Penthouse Bill Gates' Daughter Jennifer Reportedly Just Paid $51M for in a 'Paparazzi-Proof' NYC Luxury Building," Business Insider, February 25, 2023.

48. Michelle Higgins, "For the New York Condo Owner with Everything, a Million-Dollar Parking Spot," *New York Times*, September 9, 2014.

49. Steven Gaines, *The Sky's the Limit: Passion and Property in Manhattan* (New York: Hachette, 2005), 59.

50. Katherine Clarke, "Billionaires' Row Was Built for the World's Wealthiest. Has It Lived Up to Its Name?," *Wall Street Journal*, June 8, 2023.

51. Bearman, *Doormen*, 157.

52. Stefanos Chen, "The Downside of Life in a Supertall Tower: Leaks, Creaks, Breaks," *New York Times*, February 3, 2021.

53. Hilary Osborne, "Poor Doors: The Segregation of London's Inner-City Flat Dwellers," *Guardian*, July 25, 2014.

54. Adam Lusher, "Were 'Poor Doors' Added to Mixed Developments So Wealthy Residents Don't Have to Go In Alongside Social Housing Tenants?" Independent, July 25, 2014.

55. Robin Finn, "New York's Once and Future Mansions," *New York Times*, September 5, 2014.

56. Bernstein and Swan, *All the Money*, 205–6.

57. Steven Gaines, *Philistines at the Hedgerow* (New York: Little, Brown), 1998, 105–6.

58. Gaines, *Philistines*, 94–96.

59. Gaines, *Philistines*, 166.

60. Rob Larson, *Bit Tyrants: The Political Economy of Silicon Valley* (Chicago: Haymarket, 2020), chapter 6.

61. Katherine Clarke, "Mark Zuckerberg's Private Properties," *Wall Street Journal*, May 2, 2019.

62. Raphael Minder, "A Mexican Oil Chief's Hide-Out: Sea Views and 2 Golf Courses," *New York Times*, February 22, 2020.

63. Frank, *Richistan*, 13–16.

64. Frank, *Richistan*, 24.

65. Andrew Court, "'Trophy Trees' Are the New Wealth Status Symbol," *Daily Mail*, April 23, 2021.

66. David Kaplan, "The Yachting Class Sails Along," *Fortune*, April 13, 2009.

67. Bill Springer, "What's the Inside of a 350-Foot-Long Superyacht That Charters for over $2 Million per Week Really Like?," *Forbes*, August 22, 2020.

68. Nicole Aschoff, "Superyachts and the Super Rich," *Jacobin*, February 22, 2020.

69. Raphael Minder, "These Boats Are Really Big, but Barcelona Has the Room," *New York Times*, January 10, 2022.

70. Allison Morrow, "Jeff Bezos' Superyacht Is So Big It Needs Its Own Yacht," *CNN Business*, May 10, 2021.

71. Jacob Bogage, "Daniel Snyder's New $100 Million Purchase Is the First Superyacht with a Certified Imax Movie Theater," *Washington Post*, January 23, 2019.

72. Rupert Neate, "Mind My Picasso . . . Superyacht Owners Struggle to Protect Art," *Guardian*, February 2, 2019.

73. Rupert Neate, "Demand for Private Jets Soars as Rich Travelers Try to Avoid 'Mosh Pit,'" *Guardian*, September 30, 2021.

74. Benjamin Mullin, "When Private Jets Ferry Billionaires to Small-Town Idaho," *New York Times*, July 1, 2022.

75. Dana Wood, "Around the World in 24 Days: Is a Luxury 'Jet Cruise' for You?," *Wall Street Journal*, August 8, 2023.

76. James Barron, "That Noise? It's the 1%, Helicoptering Over Your Traffic Jam," *New York Times*, August 1, 2019.

77. Kenneth Chang, "There Are 2 Seats Left for This Trip to the International Space Station," *New York Times*, March 5, 2020.

78. Micah Maidenberg, "SpaceX and Axiom Launch Private Astronauts to Space Station," *Wall Street Journal*, April 8, 2022.

79. Micah Maidenberg and Doug Cameron, "Blue Origin Launch: Jeff Bezos and Crew Complete Successful Space Flight," *Wall Street Journal*, July 20, 2021.

80. John Branch and Christina Goldbaum, "A Rubik's Cube, Thick Socks and Giddy Anticipation: The Last Hours of the Titan," *New York Times*, July 2, 2023.

81. Kenneth Chang, "Jeff Bezos Picks 18-Year-Old Dutch Student for Blue Origin Rocket Launch," *New York Times*, July 15, 2021.

82. Alistair MacDonald, "Richard Branson Races Jeff Bezos to Space as COVID-19 Hits Business Back on Earth," *Wall Street Journal*, July 8, 2021.

83. Dave Sebastian and Benjamin Katz, "Richard Branson's Space Company Virgin Orbit Files for Bankruptcy," *Wall Street Journal*, April 4, 2023.

84. Luke Savage, "The Billionaire Space Race Is the Ultimate Symbol of Capitalist Decadence," *Jacobin*, July 14, 2021.

85. James Stewart, "Record Prices Mask a Tepid Market for Fine Art," *New York Times*, December 6, 2013.

86. Colin Moynihan, "Did Five Paintings Lose Their 'Oomph'? It's a $410 Million Question.," *New York Times*, November 15, 2022.

87. Nick Paumgarten, "The $40-Million Elbow," *New Yorker*, October 15, 2006.

88. Graham Bowley and Doreen Carvajal, "One of the World's Greatest Art Collections Hides behind This Fence," *New York Times*, May 28, 2016.

89. C. Wright Mills, *The Power Elite* (New York: Oxford University Press, 1956), 92.

90. Peter Wilson, "Want a Second Passport? Try Buying a House," *New York Times*, May 21, 2019.

91. Annie Lowrey, "Homeless Rates in U.S. Held Level Amid Recession, Study Says, but Big Gains Are Elusive," *New York Times*, December 10, 2012.

Chapter 3: The Classes

1. John Heilemann, *Pride Before the Fall: The Trials of Bill Gates and the End of the Microsoft Era* (New York: HarperCollins, 2001), 64.
2. Doug Henwood, "To Serve Is to Rule," *Harper's*, November 2019.
3. Edward Wolff, "Household Wealth Trends in the United States, 1962 to 2016: Has Middle Class Wealth Recovered?," National Bureau of Economic Research Working Paper No. 24085, November 2017, 16, 37.
4. Douglas Dowd, *Inequality and the Global Economic Crisis* (London: Pluto, 2009), 22.
5. Stephen Resnick and Richard Wolff, "The Diversity of Class Analyses: A Critique of Erik Olin Wright and Beyond," *Critical Sociology* 29, no. 1 (January 2003).
6. Katie Quan in Michael Zweig, ed., *What's Class Got to Do with It?: American Society in the Twenty-First Century* (Ithaca, NY: Cornell University Press, 2004), 95.
7. Matthew Josephson, *The Robber Barons: The Classic Account of the Influential Capitalists Who Transformed America's Future* (New York: Harcourt, 1934), 15.
8. Heilemann, *Pride*, 64.
9. Dowd, *Inequality*, 31.
10. C. Wright Mills, *The Power Elite* (New York: Oxford University Press, 1956), 30–31.
11. Erik Olin Wright, *Understanding Class* (London: Verso, 2015), 8.
12. Rob Larson, *Capitalism vs. Freedom: The Toll Road to Serfdom* (Alresford, UK: Zero, 2018).
13. Robin Hahnel, *The ABCs of Political Economy: A Modern Approach* (London: Pluto, 2014), 273.
14. Michael Porter and Jan Rivkin, "Prosperity at Risk: Findings of Harvard Business School's Survey on U.S. Competitiveness," Harvard Business School, January 2012, 6.
15. Aaron Bernstein, "The Wage Squeeze," *Businessweek*, July 17, 1995.
16. Eric Morath, Theo Francis, and Justin Baer, "The COVID Economy Carves Deep Divide Between Haves and Have-Nots," *Wall Street Journal*, October 5, 2020.
17. Barbara Ehrenreich, *Fear of Falling: The Inner Life of the Middle Class* (New York: Pantheon, 1989), 15.
18. Anne Case and Angus Deaton, "Life Expectancy in Adulthood Is Falling for Those without a BA Degree, but as Educational Gaps Have Widened, Racial Gaps Have Narrowed," *Proceedings of the National Academy of Sciences* 118, no. 11 (March 8, 2021).
19. David Wessel, "As Rich-Poor Gap Widens in the U.S., Class Mobility Stalls," *Wall Street Journal*, May 13, 2005.

20. David Shipler, "Total Poverty Awareness," *New York Times*, February 21, 2004.

21. Anemona Hartocollis, "A Trial about Wealth, Privilege and the Murkiness of College Admissions," *New York Times*, October 6, 2021.

22. Aatish Bhatia, Claire Cain Miller, and Josh Katz, "Study of Elite College Admissions Data Suggests Being Very Rich Is Its Own Qualification," *New York Times*, July 24, 2023.

23. Khadeeja Safdar, "On Hold for 45 Minutes? It Might Be Your Secret Customer Score," *Wall Street Journal*, November 1, 2018.

24. Paul Fussell, *Class: A Guide Through the American Status System* (New York: Simon & Schuster, 1983), 191–93.

25. Peter W. Bernstein and Annalyn Swan, *All the Money in the World: How the Forbes 400 Make—and Spend—Their Fortunes* (New York: Knopf, 2007), 188.

26. John Kampfner, *The Rich: From Slaves to Super Yachts: A 2,000-Year History* (London: Little, Brown, 2014), xiii.

27. Thorstein Veblen, *The Theory of the Leisure Class* (Oxford, UK: Oxford University Press, 2007), 131.

28. Carl Becker, "John Jay and Peter van Schaack," *Quarterly Journal of the New York State Historical Association* 1, no. 1 (October 1919): 2.

29. Josephson, *Robber Barons*, 355.

30. Stanley Aronowitz, *How Class Works: Power & Social Movement* (New Haven, CT: Yale University, 2003), 94–95.

31. Doug Henwood, "Take Me to Your Leader: The Rot of the American Ruling Class," *Jacobin*, April 27, 2021.

32. Mills, *Power Elite*, 50.

33. Henwood, "To Serve Is to Rule."

34. Larson, *Capitalism vs. Freedom*, chapter 1.

35. George Orwell, *As I Please, 1943–1945: Volume 3 of the Collected Essays, Journalism and Letters of George Orwell* (New York: Nonpareil, 2000), 118.

36. Barbara Ehrenreich, *This Land Is Their Land: Reports from a Divided Nation* (New York: Holt, 2009), 129.

37. Josephson, *Robber Barons*, 414–45.

38. Thomas Ferguson, *Golden Rule: The Investment Theory of Party Competition and the Logic of Money-Driven Political Systems* (University of Chicago Press, 1995), 8, 27.

39. David Kirkpatrick, "In a Message to Democrats, Wall St. Sends Cash to GOP," *New York Times*, February 7, 2010.

40. Jane Sasseen, "The Changes Business Wants from Obama," *Businessweek*, November 5, 2008.

41. Brendan Greeley, "Finance Executives Are Confused about Why the Nation Loathes Them," *Businessweek*, December 16, 2013.

42. Rebecca Ballhaus and Brody Mullins, "Wall Street's Donor Role Expands as Money Flows into 2016 Election," *Wall Street Journal*, February 1, 2016.

NOTES

NOTES 207

NOTES

NOTES 207

…

4.   See Barry Lynn, *Cornered: The New Monopoly Capitalism and the Economics of Destruction* (Hoboken, NJ: John Wiley, 2010).

5.   Peter Bernstein and Annalyn Swan, *All the Money in the World: How the Forbes 400 Make—and Spend—Their Fortunes* (New York: Knopf, 2007), 66.

6.   Chrystia Freeland, *Plutocrats: The Rise of the New Global Super-Rich and the Fall of Everyone Else* (New York: Penguin, 2013), 9–11.

7.   Danny Dorling, *Inequality and the 1%* (London: Verso, 2019), 44.

8.   Caroline Freund and Sarah Oliver, "The Origins of the Superrich: The Billionaire Characteristics Database," Peterson Institute for International Economics, Working Papers 16-1, February 2016.

9.   Abigail Disney, "I Was Taught From a Young Age to Protect My Dynastic Wealth," *Atlantic*, June 17, 2021.

10. Paul Piff et al., "Higher Social Class Predicts Increased Unethical Behavior," *Proceedings of the National Academy of Sciences* 109, no. 11 (February 27, 2012).

11. Jennifer Burns, *Goddess of the Market: Ayn Rand and the American Right* (New York: Oxford University Press, 2009), 177.

12. Ginia Bellafante, "The Rich Have a Coronavirus Cure: Escape from New York," *New York Times*, March 14, 2020.

13. Joshua David Stein, "The City's One-Percenters Flee the Rest of Us to the Hamptons," *New York*, March 20, 2020.

14. Kevin Quealy, "The Richest Neighborhoods Emptied Out Most as Coronavirus Hit New York City," *New York Times*, May 15, 2020.

15. Suzanne Woolley and Devon Pendleton, "Quandary for High Flyers: How to Travel Safely to Your Yacht," Bloomberg, May 22, 2020.

16. Nick Bilton, "'All These Rich People Can't Stop Themselves': The Luxe Quarantine Lives of Silicon Valley's Elite," *Vanity Fair*, August 13, 2020.

17. Rupert Neate, "Super-Rich Jet Off to Disaster Bunkers amid Coronavirus Outbreak," *Guardian*, March 11, 2020.

18. Sarah Maslin Nir and Tracey Tully, "Did New Yorkers Who Fled to Second Homes Bring the Virus?," *New York Times*, April 10, 2020.

19. Paul Sullivan, "In Pandemic, More Are Paying for Direct Access to Their Doctors," *New York Times*, August 21, 2020.

20. Gillian Friedman, "Pandemic Luxury: 'Concierge-Style' Coaches and $350 Movie Tickets," *New York Times*, July 21, 2020.

21. Ben Eisen, "In Coronavirus Recession, the Out-of-Work Turn to GoFundMe," *Wall Street Journal*, November 21, 2020.

22. Amy Gamerman, "Wealthy City Dwellers Seek Refuge from Coronavirus at Remote Ranches," *Wall Street Journal*, April 8, 2020.

23. Arundhati Roy, "The Pandemic Is a Portal," *Financial Times*, April 3, 2020.

24. Patricia Mazzei, "Everyone Wants an Antibody Test. Everyone on This Private Island Can Get One.," *New York Times*, April 14, 2020.

25. Megan Twohey, Keith Collins, and Katie Thomas, "With First Dibs on Vaccines, Rich Countries Have 'Cleared the Shelves,'" *New York Times*, December 15, 2020.

26. Bilton, "'All These Rich People.'"

27. Brian Merchant, *The One Device: The Secret History of the iPhone* (New York: Little, Brown, 2017), 190–91.

28. Janet Abbate, *Inventing the Internet* (Cambridge, MA: MIT Press, 2000), 135. The best history of the development of the Internet, filled with fascinating detail and showing consistently little involvement from the private sector.

29. James Curran, Natalie Fenton, and Des Freedman, *Misunderstanding the Internet* (New York: Routledge, 2016), 54.

30. Larson, *Bit Tyrants*, 123.

31. Freeland, *Plutocrats*, 246.

32. Luke Savage, "Do Not Welcome Our New Billionaire Overlords," *Jacobin*, November 18, 2021.

33. Bernstein and Swan, *All the Money*, 236.

34. Robert Frank, *Richistan: A Journey Through the 21st Century Wealth Boom and the Lives of the New Rich* (New York: Random House, 2007), 162.

35. Frank, *Richistan*, 159, 175–76, 178.

36. Linsey McGoey, *No Such Thing as a Free Gift: The Gates Foundation and the Price of Philanthropy* (London: Verso, 2015), 7–9.

37. John Kampfner, *The Rich: From Slaves to Super Yachts: A 2,000-Year History* (London: Little, Brown, 2014), 224–25.

38. Josephson, *Robber Barons*, 322–24.

39. Josephson, *Robber Barons*, 325.

40. James Wallace and Jim Erickson, *Hard Drive: Bill Gates and the Making of the Microsoft Empire* (New York: HarperCollins, 1992), 38.

41. Wallace and Erickson, *Hard Drive*, 211.

42. *The Simpsons*, season 9, episode 14, "Das Bus," directed by Pete Michels, written by David X. Cohen, aired February 15, 1998, on Fox, https://www.youtube.com/watch?v=H27rfr59RiE.

43. Steven Levy, "Bill Gates and President Bill Clinton on the NSA, Safe Sex, and American Exceptionalism," *Wired*, November 2013.

44. Randall Smith, "As His Foundation Has Grown, Gates Has Slowed His Donations," *New York Times* DealBook, May 26, 2014.

45. Emily Glazer, "Melinda French Gates No Longer Pledges Bulk of Her Wealth to Gates Foundation," *Wall Street Journal*, February 2, 2022.

46. Bernstein and Swan, *All the Money*, 279.

47. Donald McNeil Jr., "Gates Foundation Pledges $50 Million to Fight Ebola," *New York Times*, September 10, 2014.

48. Kampfner, *The Rich*, 342.

49. Paul Sullivan, "Private Citizen Bloomberg on Philanthropy," *New York Times*, April 25, 2014; Agustino Fontevecchia, "Bored of Philanthropy, Billionaire Mike Bloomberg Back as Chief at Bloomberg LP," *Forbes*, September 3, 2014.

50. Stephanie Strom, "Helmsley Left Dogs Billions in Her Will," *New York Times*, July 2, 2008.

51. Liz Alderman and Steven Erlanger, "As Rich Lavish Cash on Notre-Dame, Many Ask: What About the Needy?," *New York Times*, April 17, 2019.

52. Bernstein and Swan, *All the Money*, 302.

53. Jeffery Gettleman, "Meant to Keep Malaria Out, Mosquito Nets Are Used to Haul Fish In," *New York Times*, January 24, 2015.

54. Eric Wallerstein, "FTX Seeks to Recoup Sam Bankman-Fried's Charitable Donations," *Wall Street Journal*, January 7, 2023.

55. McGoey, *No Such Thing*, 31.

56. Eric Young, "Millions of American Donate through Crowdfunding Sites to Help Others Pay for Medical Bills," NORC, University of Chicago, February 19, 2020.

57. Nathan Robinson, "How Billionaires See Themselves," *Current Affairs*, January 5, 2021.

Chapter 5: The Burden

1. Lucas Chancel et al., *World Inequality Report 2022* (World Inequality Lab, 2021), 146.

2. Matthew Josephson, *The Robber Barons: The Classic Account of the Influential Capitalists Who Transformed America's Future* (New York: Harcourt, 1934), 441.

3. Chancel et al., *World Inequality Report 2022*, 133.

4. Joe Fassler, "The Superyachts of Billionaires Are Starting to Look a Lot Like Theft," *New York Times*, April 10, 2023.

5. Fassler, "Superyachts."

6. Ann Louise Bardach, "Lifestyles of the Rich and Parched," Politico, August 24, 2014.

7. Christoper Flavelle et al., "Mississippi Crisis Highlights Climate Threat to Drinking Water Nationwide," *New York Times*, September 4, 2022.

8. Andrew Court, "'Trophy Trees' Are the New Wealth Status Symbol," *Daily Mail*, April 23, 2021.

9. Peter W. Bernstein and Annalyn Swan, *All the Money in the World: How the Forbes 400 Make—and Spend—Their Fortunes* (New York: Knopf, 2007), 158.

10. Thomas Wiedmann et al., "Scientists' Warning on Affluence," *Nature Communications* 11:3107 (June 19, 2020).

11. Jamie Weinstein, "George Will Calls Global Warming 'A Religion,' 'Socialism by the Back Door,'" Daily Caller, April 27, 2014.

12. Core Writing Team, Hoesung Lee, and José Romero, eds., IPCC, 2023: Summary for Policymakers, in *Climate Change 2023: Synthesis Report. Contribution of Working Groups I, II and III to the Sixth Assessment Report of the Intergovernmental Panel on Climate Change,*(Geneva, Switzerland: IPCC, 2023), 4–5, 7.

13. Tosin Thompson, "Young People's Climate Anxiety Revealed in Landmark Survey," *Nature*, September 22, 2021.

14. Nadja Popovich and Brad Plumer, "Who Has the Most Historical Responsibility for Climate Change?," *New York Times*, November 12, 2021.

15. Rob Larson, "Trillions and Trillions: The Selective Blindness on Endless Economic Growth," *Current Affairs*, Nov/Dec 2021.

16. Chancel et al., *World Inequality Report 2022*, 129.

17. Chancel et al., *World Inequality Report 2022*, 133.

18. Chancel et al., *World Inequality Report 2022*, 135.

19. Chancel et al., *World Inequality Report 2022*, 141–42.

20. Chancel et al., *World Inequality Report 2022*, 144.

21. Lucas Chancel and Thomas Piketty, "Carbon and Inequality: From Kyoto to Paris," Paris School of Economics, November 3, 2015, 2.

22. Tim Gore, "Carbon Inequality in 2030," Oxfam, November 5, 2021, 4.

23. Gore, "Carbon Inequality," 30.

24. Matthew Huber, *Climate Change as Class War: Building Socialism on a Warming Planet* (London: Verso, 2022), 61–62.

25. Edward Wolff, "Household Wealth Trends in the United States, 1962 to 2016: Has Middle Class Wealth Recovered?," National Bureau of Economic Research Working Paper No. 24085, November 2017, 16, 37.

26. Wolff, "Household Wealth Trends," 55.

27. "The Jet Traveler Report," Wealth-X / VistaJet, 2018.

28. Robert Frank, *Richistan: A Journey Through the 21st Century Wealth Boom and the Lives of the New Rich* (New York: Random House, 2007), 133.

29. Frank, *Richistan*, 135.

30. Doug Gollan, "This Is Where You Will Find the Most Private Jets per UHNW Population," *Forbes*, August 22, 2021.

31. Stefan Gössling, "Celebrities, Air Travel, and Social Norms," *Annals of Tourism Research* 49, no. 4 (October 2019).

32. Chancel et al., *World Inequality Report 2022*, 130.

33. Bill Gates, *How to Avoid a Climate Disaster: The Solutions We Have and the Breakthroughs We Need* (New York: Knopf, 2021).

34. Yan Zhuang and Euan Ward, "Twitter Reinstates Suspended Accounts of Several Journalists," *New York Times*, December 17, 2022.

35. "Private Jets: Can the Super-Rich Supercharge Zero-Emission Aviation?," Transport & Environment, May 2021.

36. Constant Méheut, "As France Swelters, Private Jets Come Under Attack," *New York Times*, August 25, 2022.

37. Vanessa Bee, "Home For the 'Gilets Jaunes' Days," *Current Affairs*, December 10, 2018.

38. Alex Ledsom, "France's Rich Get Much Richer After Abolition of Wealth Tax," *Forbes*, October 9, 2020.

39. Chancel et al., *World Inequality Report 2022*, 128, 131.

40. George Melloan, "The Yellow Jackets Are Right About Green Policies," *Wall Street Journal*, December 16, 2018.

41. Méheut, "As France Swelters."

42. Dharna Noor, "Ban Private Jets," Gizmodo, November 1, 2021.

43. David Streitfeld and Erin Woo, "The Amazonification of Space Begins in Earnest," *New York Times*, July 21, 2021.

44. Rob Larson, *Bit Tyrants: The Political Economy of Silicon Valley* (Chicago: Haymarket, 2020), chapter 8.

45. Chancel et al., *World Inequality Report 2022*, 146.

Chapter 6: The Clans

1. John Kampfner, *The Rich: From Slaves to Super-Yachts: A 2,000-Year History* (London: Little, Brown, 2014), 362.

2. Kampfner, *The Rich*, xxv.

3. Rob Larson, "Not Too Big Enough," *Dollars & Sense*, July/August 2010.

4. Rebecca Davis O'Brien, "Epstein's Longtime Pilot Said the Cockpit Door Stayed Closed on the Financier's Planes," *New York Times*, November 30, 2021.

5. Khadeeja Safdar and Emily Glazer, "Jeffrey Epstein Appeared to Threaten Bill Gates over Microsoft Co-Founder's Affair with Russian Bridge Player," *Wall Street Journal*, May 21, 2023.

6. Richard Chang, "How the World's Billionaires Got So Rich 2023," *Forbes*, April 9, 2023.

7. "Everybody Wants to Rule the World," *Economist*, November 27, 2014.

8. Don Clark and Robert McMillan, "Facebook, Amazon and Other Tech Giants Tighten Grip on Internet Economy," *Wall Street Journal*, November 6, 2015.

9. Lucas Chancel et al., *World Inequality Report 2022* (World Inequality Lab, 2021), 34.

10. Kampfner, *The Rich*, 286.

11. Abdulhadi Khalaf, Omar AlShehabi, and Adam Hanieh, eds., *Transit States: Labour, Migration and Citizenship in the Gulf* (London: Pluto, 2015), 4, 16.

12. Christina Goldbaum, "His Estate Has 3 Swimming Pools and a Stable. He Says He's Not Rich.," *New York Times*, December 10, 2022.

13. Kampfner, *The Rich*, 291.

14. Stephen Kalin, "Saudi Royals Are Selling Homes, Yachts and Art as Crown Prince Cuts Income," *Wall Street Journal*, April 24, 2022.

15. Robert Worth, "The Dark Reality Behind Saudi Arabia's Utopian Dreams," *New York Times Magazine*, January 28, 2021.

16. Rory Smith, "Saudi Arabia, Newcastle and Soccer's Worship of Money," *New York Times*, October 8, 2021.

17. Warren Strobel, "CIA Concludes Saudi Journalist Was Killed on Crown Prince's Order," *Wall Street Journal*, November 17, 2018.

18. Justin Scheck, Bradley Hope, and Summer Said, "Bezos, Saudi Prince Suffer Bitter Split," *Wall Street Journal*, January 27, 2020.

19. Kampfner, *The Rich*, 308.

20. Chancel et al., *World Inequality Report 2022*, 34.

21. Kampfner, *The Rich*, 313.

22. Kevin Koenig, "How Much Does That Oligarch's Yacht Actually Cost?," *New York Times*, September 2, 2022.
23. Rory Jones, "Russian Oligarchs' Private Jets Find Refuge in Dubai but Can't Leave," *Wall Street Journal*, April 9, 2022.
24. Anton Troianovski and Jack Ewing, "How Russia's Rich Get Their Luxuries Now," *New York Times*, May 11, 2023.
25. Jared Malsin and Elvan Kivilcim, "Superyachts, Seaside Apartments and Suitcases Full of Cash: Russians Pour Money into Turkey," *Wall Street Journal*, April 7, 2022.
26. Raphael Minder and Barbara Erling, "Affluent Ukrainian Refugees Boost Polish Luxury Businesses," *Financial Times*, March 3, 2023.
27. Laurie Burkitt, "Rolling Out the Red Carpet," *Wall Street Journal*, October 23, 2013.
28. Chancel et al., *World Inequality Report 2022*, 213.
29. Branko Milanovic, *Global Inequality: A New Approach for the Age of Globalization* (Cambridge, MA: Harvard University Press, 2016), 178–79.
30. Michael Forsythe, "Billionaire Lawmakers Ensure the Rich Are Represented in China's Legislature," *New York Times*, March 2, 2015.
31. Kampfner, *The Rich*, 325–26.
32. Stella Yifan Xie, "Xi Jinping's 'Common Prosperity' Was Everywhere, but China Backed Off," *Wall Street Journal*, April 3, 2022.
33. Chancel et al., *World Inequality Report 2022*, 34.
34. Nick Kostov and Stacy Meichtry, "The World Richest Person Auditions His Five Children to Run LVMH, the Luxury Empire," *Wall Street Journal*, April 19, 2023.
35. David de Jong, *Nazi Billionaires: The Dark History of Germany's Wealthiest Dynasties* (New York: HarperCollins, 2022), 6.
36. Andrew Hill, "Chair of the 'Firm,'" *Financial Times*, September 10–11, 2022.
37. Danny Dorling, *Inequality and the 1%* (London: Verso, 2019), 13–14.
38. World Bank, *Global Development Finance 2012* (World Bank, 2012), 1.
39. Vijay Prashad, "The IMF Is Utterly Indifferent to the Pain It's Causing," ZNet, October 17, 2019.
40. Robin Hahnel, *Panic Rules!: Everything You Need to Know about the Global Economy* (Cambridge, MA: South End, 1999), ix.
41. Jonathan Ostry, Prakash Loungani, and Davide Furceri, "Neoliberalism: Oversold?," *Finance & Development* 53, no. 2 (June 2016).
42. Saeed Shah, "Pakistan Offers Sharp Shifts to Win IMF Bailout," *Wall Street Journal*, July 1, 2019.
43. Saeed Shah, "'The Middle-Class Person Is Dying.' Pakistan's Tax Push Is Deflating Its Leader's Political Base.," *Wall Street Journal*, October 17, 2019.
44. "Food in the Wrong Places," *Financial Times*, September 4, 1965.
45. James Morgan, "Rip van Winkle's New Economic Order: The Fall of the Soviet Bloc Has Left the IMF and G7 to Rule the World and Create a New Imperial Age," *Financial Times*, April 26, 1992.

Chapter 7: The Plan

1. Matthew Josephson, *The Robber Barons: The Classic Account of the Influential Capitalists Who Transformed America's Future* (New York: Harcourt, 1934), 374.

2. Chrystia Freeland, *Plutocrats: The Rise of the New Global Super-Rich and the Fall of Everyone Else* (New York: Penguin, 2013), 240.

3. Norman Finkelstein, *What Gandhi Says: About Nonviolence, Resistance and Courage* (New York: OR Books, 2012), 65.

4. "Most See Inequality Growing, but Partisans Differ over Solutions," Pew Research Center, January 23, 2014.

5. Rich Morin, "Rising Share of Americans See Conflict Between Rich and Poor," Pew Research Center, January 11, 2012.

6. Max Ehrenfreund, "A Majority of Millennials Now Reject Capitalism, Poll Shows," *Washington Post*, April 26, 2016.

7. Hannah Hartig, "Stark Partisan Divisions in Americans' Views of 'Socialism,' 'Capitalism,'" Pew Research Center, June 25, 2019.

8. "In Their Own Words: Behind Americans' Views of 'Socialism' and 'Capitalism,'" Pew Research Center, October 7, 2019.

9. Frank Newport, "Democrats More Positive about Socialism Than Capitalism," Gallup, August 13, 2018.

10. J. Baxter Oliphant, "Top Tax Frustrations for Americans: The Feeling That Some Corporations, Wealthy People Don't Pay Fair Share," Pew Research Center, April 7, 2023.

11. Felix Salmon, "America's Continued Move toward Socialism," Axios, June 25, 2021.

12. Carl Beijer, "Socialism's Base Is the Poor, and Capitalism's Base Is the Rich," carlbeijer.com, October 27, 2022.

13. "Millennial Socialism," *Economist*, February 16, 2019.

14. Rob Larson, *Capitalism vs. Freedom: The Toll Road to Serfdom* (Alresford, UK: Zero Books, 2018), introduction and chapter 1.

15. "Life, liberty and the pursuit of property," *Economist*, February 16, 2019.

16. Glenn Hubbard, "Even My Business-School Students Have Doubts About Capitalism," *Atlantic*, January 2, 2022.

17. Josephson, *Robber Barons*, 227.

18. Josephson, *Robber Barons*, 372.

19. Josephson, *Robber Barons*, 421.

20. Kris Maher, "Strikes Becoming More Common Amid Inflation, Tight Labor Market," *Wall Street Journal*, September 16, 2022.

21. Noam Scheiber, "How the Pandemic Has Added to Labor Unrest," *New York Times*, November 1, 2021.

22. David Harrison, "Amazon Workers' Union Victory Bolsters Revitalized Labor Movement," *Wall Street Journal*, April 2, 2022.

23. Noam Scheiber, "Companies Are Taking a Harder Line on Union Organizers, Workers Say," *New York Times*, May 22, 2023.

24. Noam Scheiber, "Supreme Court Backs Employer in Suit over Strike Losses," *New York Times*, June 1, 2023.

25. Adam Cohen, *Supreme Inequality: The Supreme Court's Fifty-Year Battle for a More Unjust America* (New York: Penguin, 2020), 244.

26. Paul Berger, "New Ports Contract Would Raise Pay 32%, Bring Dockworkers $70 Million in Bonuses," *Wall Street Journal*, June 15, 2023.

27. Kris Maher, "Strikes Becoming More Common amid Inflation, Tight Labor Market," *New York Times*, September 16, 2022.

28. Noam Scheiber and Niraj Chokshi, "Workers Say Railroads' Efficiency Push Became Too Much," *New York Times*, September 15, 2022.

29. Maher, "Strikes."

30. Kris Maher, "Unions Eye L.A. Charter Schools," *Wall Street Journal*, November 16, 2015.

31. Noam Scheiber, "The Revolt of the College-Educated Working Class," *New York Times*, April 28, 2022.

32. Heather Haddon, "Starbucks Closing Some Stores, Citing Safety Concerns in Certain Cafes," *Wall Street Journal*, July 12, 2022.

33. Karen Weise and Michael Corkery, "Amazon Workers Vote Down Union Drive at Alabama Warehouse," *New York Times*, April 9, 2021.

34. Lauren Kaori Gurley, "A Homeless Amazon Warehouse Worker in New York City Tells Her Story," *Vice*, June 18, 2021.

35. Noam Scheiber and Karen Weise, "Amazon Loses Bid to Overturn Union Victory at Staten Island Warehouse," *New York Times*, January 11, 2023.

36. Sebastian Herrera, "Unionization Stalls at Amazon as Turnover, Company Efforts Stymie Activism," *Wall Street Journal*, December 28, 2022.

37. Sebastian Herrera, "Amazon Workers Reject Union in Vote at Upstate New York Warehouse," *Wall Street Journal*, October 18, 2022.

38. Salvador Rodriguez, "Apple Employees at Maryland Store Vote to Unionize," *Wall Street Journal*, June 18, 2022.

39. Jack Ewing, "Tesla Workers in Buffalo Begin Union Drive," *New York Times*, February 14, 2023.

40. Noam Scheiber, "Video Game Workers Get a Union Foothold at Microsoft," *New York Times*, January 3, 2023.

41. Mike Colias, "Detroit Is Paying Up to End the UAW Strike. Now Carmakers Will Live with the Costs.," *Wall Street Journal*, October 30, 2023.

42. Nora Eckert and Mike Colias, "Three Young Activists Who Never Worked in an Auto Factory Helped Deliver Huger Win for the UAW," *Wall Street Journal*, October 30, 2023.

43. John Kampfner, *The Rich: From Slaves to Super-Yachts: A 2,000-Year History* (London: Little, Brown, 2014), 202–203.

44. Kirsten Grind et al., "Elon Musk Is Planning a Texas Utopia—His Own Town," *Wall Street Journal*, March 9, 2023.

45. Kathy Chu, "China Loses Edge on Labor Costs," *Wall Street Journal*, December 3, 2015.

46. Stanley Aronowitz, *How Class Works: Power & Social Movement* (New Haven, CT: Yale University, 2003), 102–103.

47. Mica Rosenberg, Kristina Cooke, and Joshua Schneyer, "Child Workers Found throughout Hyundai-Kia Supply Chain in Alabama," Reuters, December 16, 2022.

48. Hannah Dreier, "Alone and Exploited, Migrant Children Work Brutal Jobs Across the U.S.," *New York Times*, February 25, 2023.

49. Luis Feliz Leon, "Slingshot: Children on the Killing Floor," *Labor Notes*, May 25, 2023.

50. Adolfo Flores and Jennifer Calfas, "States Look to Ease Some Child-Labor Laws amid Tight Market," *Wall Street Journal*, March 10, 2023.

51. Jason Riley, "A Little Work Never Hurt Anyone—Including Teenagers," *Wall Street Journal*, April 11, 2023.

52. Taylor Giorno, "'Midterm Spending Spree': Cost of 2022 Federal Elections Tops $8.9 Billion, a New Midterm Record," OpenSecrets, February 7, 2023; "2020 Presidential Race," OpenSecrets, https://www.opensecrets.org/2020-presidential-race.

53. Larry Bartels, "Economic Inequality and Political Representation," Russell Sage Foundation, November 2002.

54. Paul Kiel, "How Harlan Crow Slashed His Tax Bill by Taking Clarence Thomas on Superyacht Cruises," ProPublica, July 17, 2023.

55. Laura Meckler and Richard Rubin, "Democrats' Shift Left Aids Sanders," *Wall Street Journal*, February 8, 2016.

56. Kirk Johnson, "A Rare Elected Voice for Socialism Pledges to Be Heard in Seattle," *New York Times*, December 28, 2013.

57. Peter Robison, "Occupy Tastes Rare Success in Rise of Seattle Socialist," Bloomberg, March 12, 2014.

58. John Burn-Murdoch, "Why Are Americans Dying So Young?," *Financial Times*, March 30, 2023.

59. Bradley Jones, "Increasing Share of Americans Favor a Single Government Program to Provide Health Care Coverage," Pew Research Center, September 29, 2020.

60. Carl Beijer, "The Bernie Bump Is Over," carlbeijer.com, October 26, 2022.

61. Albert Einstein, "Why Socialism?" *Monthly Review*, May 1949.

62. Matthew Miles Goodrich, "The Forgotten Socialist History of Martin Luther King Jr.," *In These Times*, January 15, 2018.

63. George Orwell, "Why I Write," *A Collection of Essays* (Orlando, FL: Harcourt Brace, 1981), 314.

64. George Orwell, *The Road to Wigan Pier* (Orlando, FL: Harcourt, 1958), 216.

65. Janet Adamy, "Most Americans Doubt Their Children Will Be Better Off, WSJ-NORC Poll Finds," *Wall Street Journal*, March 24, 2023.

66. "Red Cross Launches Food Aid Campaign for Britain," BBC News, October 11, 2023.

67. Mike Dorning, "Lines Stretch Down the Block at Food Banks as Costs Go

Up and Pandemic Aid Expires," Bloomberg, May 7, 2023.

68. Patrick Tyler, "A New Power in the Streets," *New York Times*, February 17, 2003.

69. Nick Kostov and Stacy Meichtry, "LVMH's Paris Headquarters Stormed by Protestors," *Wall Street Journal*, April 13, 2023.

70. Annie Massa and Jack Witzig, "Musk, Zuckerberg Lead a $852 Billion Surge among World's Richest People," Bloomberg, July 3, 2023.

71. Gerard Baker, "Aristocrats Face the Pitchforks," *Wall Street Journal*, January 17, 2017.

72. Olúfẹ́mi O. Táíwò, *Elite Capture: How the Powerful Took Over Identity Politics (And Everything Else)* (Chicago: Haymarket, 2022), 114.

73. Frederick Douglass in Philip S. Foner and Yuval Taylor, eds., *Frederick Douglass: Selected Speeches and Writings* (Chicago: Chicago Review Press, 1999), 367.

INDEX

Figures are indexed by the page number followed by f.

ABOUT THE AUTHOR

Rob Larson is a professor of economics at Tacoma Community College and author of *Bit Tyrants: The Political Economy of Silicon Valley* and *Capitalism vs. Freedom*. He writes for *Jacobin* and *Dollars & Sense*, and is the House Economist for *Current Affairs*. He lives in Tacoma, Washington.